Bless Back

Thank Those Who Shaped Your Life

JULIE SAFFRIN

Sandy —
It's been a pleasure
to get to know
you! —

Enjoy

Julie Saffrin

Request for information should be addressed to the publisher,
Ottertail Press, PO Box 48313, Minneapolis, Minnesota 55448

Edited by Trai Cartwright, Fort Collins, Colorado
Designed by Angie Hughes, Angie's Creative, www.AngiesCreative.com
Author photo, Scott Knutson, InsideOut Studios, Eden Prairie, Minnesota

ISBN-13: 978-0615593951   ISBN-10: 061559395X   Price: $14.99

For information about this book in an e-book format, please go to
www.BlessBack.com

To my parents, Donald and Carol Trewartha,
Thank you for modeling how to BlessBack early in my life

And to my husband, Rick, and sons Sam, Joe and Jake
You are my greatest treasures

Acknowledgments: With Thanks

Someone once said that the journey of art is a million miles. In the writing of *BlessBack: Thank Those Who Shaped Your Life*, I encountered many people in my travels whose creativity and generous hearts helped me arrive at a finished manuscript.

Most especially, I would like to thank the people who allowed me to tell their beautiful stories. Your BlessBacks inspired me as I wrote them and relived them during the editing process. No doubt, they will inspire those who read them, too. You are all amazing innovators of the kind of change you wish to see in the world. Thanks for all your encouraging notes to me along the way. They meant so much and kept me writing. And Harry, at 101, you continually amaze me for your enthusiasm about life. Richard Hargesheimer, thank you for giving me permission to use Fred's story. I hope the upcoming movie based on his life takes an Oscar, for your father was an amazing man. Nelly Trocmé Hewett, it was a pleasure to meet you and your help on Chapter 7 was invaluable.

To my writer friends Jane Kise, Joy DeKok, Sheri Jacobs, Gloria Plaisted, Tim Remington, Ron Stanchfield, De Brandt, Nancy Jobe, and Barbara Majchrzak. Your guidance, prodding and encouraging me to let my writing voice be heard kept me going, even when I couldn't see the way forward. And to those trailblazers who went before me in the publishing arena, thank you for paving the way for me to get there, too.

To Trai Cartwright. When I boarded a plane to Fort Collins, I had no idea that meeting you would not only help me re-conceive my book, but help me accomplish the task. Thank you for giving great directions.

To Angie Hughes. It has been said that if there had been no Dwight Moody, there'd have been no Billy Graham. In my instance, had there been no *Sister*, there would not have been a great book cover. Thank you for taking the time to read the manuscript and grasp its meaning so you could let your creative talents shine into a beautiful work of art. Thanks, too, for tolerating editing changes.

To my family, Sam, Joe and Jake. I could not have accomplished this dream without your allowing me the space and time to accomplish it. To my husband Rick. Thank you for letting me be me and offering your encouragement, love and support to help me realize this dream.

To my friends. Thank you for asking, "How's your book coming?" By asking, you showed me that you believed in me and helped me see this project through to its end. Each one of you mean the world to me.

To the 88th Street Pussycats. Cheryl, Cindy, Sherry and Sue. I am so thankful God gave me each one of you to accompany me on life's adventures. May our future bring more laughter than tears, unending monthly dinners and new wineries to visit.

And finally, to Pat Fatchett, the one who started me on the writing path. Thanks for being the world's best seventh grade teacher and for your encouragement. You were, and always will be, the reason I have the courage to write.

Author's Note:

The personal stories in this book appear
with consent of the people involved.

Names have been changed when requested.

Stories are for those late hours in the night
when you wonder how you got from where you were to where you are now.
Stories are for directing the past to the future.

— Tim O'Brien

Summing it all up, friends,
I'd say you'll do best by filling your minds and meditating on things
true,
noble,
reputable,
authentic,
compelling,
gracious
— the best, not the worst;
— the beautiful, not the ugly;
— things to praise, not things to curse.

... I do want you to experience the blessing that issues from generosity.

— Paul of Tarsus, to the Philippians

Table of Contents

PART ONE: WHAT IS A BLESSBACK?

Chapter One: Mind the Gap 15

Chapter Two: Eraser Man 23

 Note to Self: Illuminators of Kindness 28

Chapter Three: My BlessBack Journey 31

 Note to Self: Courage 40

PART TWO: WHY A BLESSBACK IS BENEFICIAL

Chapter Four: Building a Better You 47

 Note to Self: Life Forces 54

Chapter Five: Building Up and Blessing Others 58

 Note to Self: A Directional Pause 77

Chapter Six: BlessBacks Build Community 81

 Note to Self: Living Within Your Harvest 94

Chapter Seven: BlessBacks Build a Better World 97

 Note to Self: Conspiracy of Goodness 113

Chapter Eight: Why We Hesitate to Give BlessBacks 117
 Note to Self: Coastliners 127

Chapter Nine: When the Person You Want to BlessBack
 Has Memory Loss or Has Passed Away 131

Chapter Ten: Regrets in Life: Using BlessBacks to Restore 140

Chapter Eleven: When Relationships are Estranged 147

PART THREE: HOW TO DO A BLESSBACK

Chapter Twelve: A BlessBack Starter Kit 153

Chapter Thirteen: Giving a BlessBack Through Words 160

Chapter Fourteen: Do a BlessBack Act 175

Chapter Fifteen: Give a BlessBack Through Gifts 189

Chapter Sixteen: A BlessBack Meal 195

Chapter Seventeen: The Glory Jar 202

APPENDIX: 120 ADDITIONAL WAYS TO BLESSBACK

A. BlessBacks with Words 211

B. BlessBack Acts 213

C. BlessBacks with Gifts 217

D. BlessBacks in Special Circumstances 221

NOTES 223

REFERENCES 231

PART ONE

What is a BlessBack?

CHAPTER ONE

Mind the Gap

Courteous conductors and porters
are at the service of all Pullman passengers
and they are glad to render assistance and furnish information to travelers.

— From The Pullman Company, Chicago

I collected my luggage from Heathrow's customs and rolled it toward London's underground subway system. As I crossed to the train, a recorded man's voice over a loud speaker told me to "mind the gap" — that space between land and rail.

Funny what happens when you lift your foot from land. You put yourself at risk. You trust the train, signals, system, and brakes all to work. If they do, you are transported to a different place.

I promise you an exhilarating, life-changing journey, on the condition that you time-travel with your memories and board the train. I will sweeten the offer. You can also expect to be:

happier
healthier
less stressed
more in control of your life
empowered
less lonely
and feel like you matter . . .

. . . Will you mind the gap, take a deep breath and risk it?

I promise you an exhilarating, life-changing journey, on the condition that you time-travel with your memories and board the train.

I'm glad you chose to board. No longer are you content that you made it another day above the topsoil. You're up for an adventure. You want to take a trip. What lies between these pages sends you on a voyage, one that will give you meaning, make a difference in your life, and as you discover yourself and your past, will give meaning to others and make a difference in their lives, too.

You are on a BlessBack® journey that really is the story of you and your importance to the world.

BLESSBACK: WHAT IS IT?

Before we depart, we need to learn a few basic definitions.

A BlessBack gives thanks back to someone who has had a positive influence in one's life. It is an exchange of blessing between two parties: the giver and the receiver. As you live the BlessBack life, you will discover that at various times you may be a giver and at other times a receiver; sometimes you may experience both giving and receiving at the same time.

BlessBacks are different from random acts of kindness. Most often, a random act of kindness is being kind to someone in a spontaneous way.

A BlessBack, on the other hand, specifically directs and gives a blessing to someone in your past who was or is significant to you. It has two parts. The first part asks you to examine your life — from as long ago as when you were a child to as recently as yesterday — and look for the people who were or are a positive influence. The second part involves connecting with these influential people to give your thanks and telling them specifically how they made your life better. Instead of paying the kindness forward, a BlessBack pays your thanks backward to the person who made a difference in your life. These people are points-of-light people because an element of their attitude, personality, or character affected you in such a way as to stay in your memory. Points-of-light people may be someone who changed your day, your year, or even your life.

Life is a banquet, and most poor suckers are starving to death.

—Rosalind Russell

POINTS-OF-LIGHT PEOPLE

Points-of-light people illuminate the way for us, whether they do so by helping, teaching, respecting, guiding or offering a course correction. Perhaps someone gave you sound advice on your next career move. Maybe a friend gave you a place to live when you were between homes. Perhaps an uncle, by taking you to a foreign country, helped broaden your worldview and opened your eyes to other cultures. Perhaps someone stepped in and offered advice before you made a huge mistake. Maybe you received comfort from a friend after a loved one died or you are in the profession you are in because of a great teacher's guidance.

Points-of-light people show the way at life's crossroads. They make a difference in our lives. They help us see in a new way. They are our illuminators, lighting up an ideal and causing us to pause, pivot, retreat or advance. Illuminators can give short bright bursts of light or provide a beacon for a lifetime.

> *Points-of-light people illuminate the way for us, whether they do so by helping, teaching, respecting, guiding or offering a course correction.*

One of my tenderest BlessBacks was two sentences. The friend wrote, "I cannot compare the way you care for me to anything else I have ever experienced. You will never know how secure you make me feel."

Her words have kept me focused on the way I want to live.

All of us have dreams, hopes and goals. There are so many marvelous ways we can give someone a good day if we will only "kindle enthusiasm," as Oswald Chambers said. *Kindle* is a verb; used with an object it means "to set fire to." When points-of-light people give us a BlessBack, they stoke the fire of our hearts. Their encouragement in seeing something good in us spurs us on to be better people.

BLESSBACK IN THE SMALL MOMENTS

A BlessBack can make its greatest impact when given to those who had a life-changing effect on us, but a BlessBack also is for the moments when someone's good work in the world moves you.

When my son Jake was ten, he had a homework assignment to write a thank-you letter to a military veteran. He wrote a relative who, in 1968, enlisted into the marines.

Dear George,
Thank you very much for your service to our country
as a marine during the Vietnam War. Happy Veteran's Day!
Sincerely, Jake

A reply came two weeks later.

Dear Jake,
Thank you very much for your nice note. No one has ever
thanked me for my service to our country. Thanks for writing.
Hope to see you and your family soon.
Semper Fi, George

A BlessBack honors others. BlessBacks can be great or small. Best of all, they are for everyone and cost little, except time.

A *Los Angeles Times* reporter received an email thanking her for her tribute to the dancer and actress Cyd Charisse. The reporter responded back to the reader the next day. "Thank you for taking the time to write. You wouldn't believe the mean mail I get."

BlessBacks affect not only individuals but also marriages, families, neighborhoods, communities, schools and work places. They can build a better world of goodness and gratefulness, one person at a time. All it takes is to begin with "Thank you for ..."

Life's uncertainty is certain, yet we can lighten another's load. Words heal. Words break down the walls and fences we build between each other. When we BlessBack, we give others a momentary respite from their daily lives; their own journey through life becomes relevant to their lives today. Whether spoken or written, BlessBacks empower and encourage. They create exponential and ever-expanding connections of gratitude.

Whether spoken or written, BlessBacks empower and encourage. They create exponential and ever-expanding connections of gratitude.

"Life is short," wrote Henri-Frederic Amiel, "and we have never too much time for gladdening the hearts of those who are travelling the dark journey with us. Oh be swift to love, make haste to be kind."

You cannot change the laws of gravity. You may not be able to change your financial situation or stop from facing a life crisis, but you can reframe the realities in which you, and others around you, live.

You have it easily within your power
to increase the sum total of the world's happiness now.

— Dale Carnegie

When we think about how grateful we are for what someone has done for us, but keep it inside, it only benefits us. While this may self-satisfy, this kind of satisfaction does not stay for long and it does nothing to change the world. *Gratify*, according to Webster, is from the Old French *gratus* (pleasing) and the Latin *facere* (make) and means to satisfy and to do. Gratify is a call to action and that is what a BlessBack is all about.

Andre Agassi knew this. After the last match of his professional tennis career he said to the crowd,

"The scoreboard said I lost today, but what the scoreboard doesn't say is what it is I have found. Over the last twenty-one years, I have found loyalty. You have pulled for me on the court and also in life. I have found inspiration. You have willed me to succeed. Sometimes even in my lowest moments, I've found generosity. You have given me your shoulders to stand on to reach for my dreams, dreams I could never have reached without you … I will take you and the memory of you with me for the rest of my life."[1]

People are a part of life's tapestry and when someone specifically gives thanks to another, both lives are the richer for it.

Take time to look back and explore where you received goodness from others and you will find positive memories — what Wordsworth called "spots of time." If you offer a BlessBack to people who have made a difference in your life, you will not only deliver joy into their common days, but your action will bring joy into your life, too. If you believe and act upon BlessBack's transforming powers, you will rattle the globe in a good way.

In the beautiful, thought-provoking movie *Get Low*, Robert Duvall plays Felix Bush, an old, self-described hermit who knows townsfolk spin rumors about him. When a friend dies without Felix expressing how he felt about him, Felix decides to put on his own funeral party while he is still alive. He knows people want to discuss past events, and he wants to hear their stories, good or bad. Felix's reasoning, he tells the perplexed owner of Quinn Funeral Home, is that he has heard people eulogized at funerals. "I remember wishing," he tells Quinn, "they could hear all the beautiful things people said about them."

We wait until people are gone to honor and thank them for being a part of our lives when we could tell them before they die how we feel.

This book challenges you to give living eulogies. It will guide you by sharing examples of others' BlessBack stories, and give you insights and ideas of how to offer thanks in a meaningful way to those who have illuminated your life.

NOTE TO SELF

For each leg of their journey, navigators use the tides, weather and maps to chart their course. This book is about taking a life-changing journey. To have a successful voyage, one must not only have a desire to change one's direction but also have the equipment necessary to arrive at the destination. Included in this book are *Note to Self* sections to give you the tools needed on your quest for change. These self-study places are for you to write your feelings as you read. They are designed to cause you to think about your life and those people in it whom you want to BlessBack.

Each *Note to Self* has five elements. They are an *ideal*, a *look back*, an *invitation*, a *BlessBack course of action*, and a *benediction*. An *ideal* is something of value to pursue, maybe a feeling, a virtue or a goal. The *look back* asks you to find the visible ideal in your life and write about the person who demonstrated it to you. The *invitation* poses questions for reflection on the ideal and challenges you to apply the ideal to your life. The *BlessBack course of action* provides writing space for you to get started implementing the ideal. Use the *benediction* as a prayer or an affirmation to empower and encourage you to act.

Take the time to write your responses for each of the *Note to Self* elements in the space provided as you will use what you write later. You can do the *Note to Self* section all in one day, or you may find you want to give more time — perhaps one section daily — to your writing. The idea is for you to reflect on the questions as you think about your life.

Where you decide to time-travel with your BlessBacks is up to you.

You might give your first BlessBack to someone you just met. Others of you may take a window seat and mentally meander back through your lifetime, and let your memories tell you to whom you want to BlessBack first.

Let the stories and your notes within this book's pages carry you to a changed life, a joy-filled life. Use these pages as a road map to find your redemptive roots. Let them transport you to a more thankful, purpose-filled, and affirmed you.

Open your passport. Let's begin.

Use these pages as a road map to find your redemptive roots. Let them transport you to a more thankful, purpose-filled, and affirmed you.

For my part,
I travel not to go anywhere, but to go.
I travel for travel's sake.
The great affair is to move;
to feel the needs and hitches
of our life more nearly.

— Robert Louis Stevenson
Notes From a Traveler Afar

CHAPTER TWO
Eraser Man

There are very few human beings who receive the truth,
complete and staggering, by instant illumination.
Most of them acquire it fragment by fragment,
on a small scale, by successive developments…

— Anaïs Nin

You are here to enrich the world,
and you impoverish yourself if you forget the errand.

— Woodrow Wilson

My two brothers, Mark and Steve, and I went to an elementary school three blocks from our house in Bloomington, Minnesota. Our best memory is when our teachers asked us to clean the chalkboard erasers. As a kid, cleaning erasers at River Ridge Elementary School meant escape from class at the time of day when you ached for the school bell to ring. No one in authority questioned your presence in the empty halls at ten minutes to three because they saw you carrying erasers like logs to a campfire.

Our school was round and classrooms had doorless, wide entries so when you walked by, students looked at you with eraser-envy. One smirk was enough to rub it in that your day was done. Another twenty paces took you past the lunchroom where Miss Stella counted lunch tickets and the day's earnings, past the nurse's office and who was in trouble in Principal Tufino's office. Finally you reached that hallowed, mysterious place that housed the cleaning machines — the custodian's office.

Our custodian Mr. Driste, or "Harry," as he preferred, reminded me of a mix between a tall, happy Mr. Magoo and G.I. Joe. He had a shiny head, was trim, and wore wire-rimmed glasses, grey shirt and pants, and heavy boots that propelled his long stride. A keyring clipped to his belt loop had a wire zipline that seemed to stretch the gym's width.

Harry could have cleaned the erasers himself; instead he remembered he was once a kid at the end of a school day and figured out a way for students to escape. For the kids, it was heaven; for Harry, it was a chance to show kids his working world — one in which he was immensely proud.

Unlike teachers and their private lounge, Harry welcomed us into his world. Once inside Harry's "office," on the side of the gym, you not only felt safe because it was near the bomb shelter, but you felt secure because Harry was there and Harry could do anything. In his soft-spoken manner, he showed children how to clean erasers, both the black-felt version and the longer chamois-and-rubber ones.

His office smelled like soap, chemicals and wax; it held tools and equipment that intrigued. He used different cleaning products than Mom used. There was no Mr. Clean, Janitor in a Drum, or Big Wally on his shelves but industrial-looking cans with images of pirate flags and scary letters that reminded me of the Soviet Union. His brooms looked different, too. They were short-bristled and wide. Two damp spaghetti mops hung in a neat row next to a floor drain. He had a galvanized aluminum mop bucket on wheels with a built-in squeegee lever.

Cleaning erasers took only two minutes — never long enough. We just didn't want to leave Harry's office. Students loved Harry. I loved him because of the pride he took in caring for the school gymnasium floor. Every week he buffed it to squeaky perfection. He also learned all four hundred of our names, no small feat at seventy-three. He wanted to know us. He illuminated us, made us feel visible.

For some, Harry was a surrogate parent. For kids whose parents didn't come to band concerts, Harry stayed late, leaned against his office door in the gymnasium, and sipped coffee from the cup of his Thermos, smiling approval at our grunts and squeaks.

As kids do, we moved on to junior high. In ninth grade, we learned Harry planned to retire at the end of the school year. A handful of kids from my neighborhood made a giant card. We drew a fish with big scales, signed our good lucks, and gave it to him. He was blurry-eyed as he thanked us.

We graduated high school. Our elementary school closed due to low enrollment. A corporation bought the building. We went to college, got jobs, married and had kids.

Life advanced the years. Twenty-five, in fact.

My brother Mark fell in love with Jenny in 1998. They went to visit Jenny's grandfather and his wife at their home a couple hours west of the Twin Cities.

Jenny's grandpa introduced himself to Mark as Harry Driste.

Flabbergasted, Mark told him about being a student at River Ridge and asked if he had worked there.

Harry didn't answer. Instead, he said he wanted to show Mark something in his finished basement. Mark followed Harry. Hanging on the center of a paneled wall was a two- by three-foot manila-colored poster with a giant fish drawn on it. "Harry's Fisherman Code: Early to bed, early to rise. Fish with flies, and make up lies!" was on the top half. On the bottom half, in colored pencils and magic markers, were written our childhood farewells.

Mark called later that evening. "You won't believe it," he said and told me the story.

Mark and Jenny married. Years later, Jenny's daughter, Emma, graduated in 2007 from high school and Jenny's parents drove to Paynesville to bring Harry, then ninety-seven, and his wife to the graduation open house in Minneapolis.

When I entered Mark's house, Harry was in an arm chair and he'd brought the retirement poster from twenty-five years ago and held it up to show me. He still had the same smile.

We hugged and talked about River Ridge. "That was the best place I ever worked," he said. "You kids always treated me so nice."

He opened the big card. I saw my handwriting tucked in a corner. "To the best janitor around," it said. "Thanks for making River Ridge the cleanest school in town." I looked at the circle of signatures — some of whom were still my best friends. My brothers had signed it, as had neighbor kids who had moved, and another, Vicki Davis, who had died at eighteen. All of us, just teens at the time, had left our thanks and wishes for his happiness in retirement.

Our simply constructed send-off held such meaning for Harry; it was a visible affirmation in his retirement that he had lived a meaningful life. It told him that his presence at school had a positive impact on the students and we, in turn, had illuminated him.

I am still friends with a handful of my elementary school friends. In fact, we've known each other since I was four. Sue Koscienski, Cheryl Yeager, Sherry Dircks, Cindy Nelson, and I have learned much from one another through the years. As young children, we practiced our weddings with Bridal Doll Box paper dolls. As teens, they counseled me when my heartthrob, Bobby Sherman, who'd asked in a song if I loved him, married someone else. We weathered the drama of high school together. We celebrated our marriages, our children's births and their graduations, and we've sat by each other's sides as we've said loving good-byes to those we've lost. Early on, Cindy named us the 88th Street Pussycats. We meet every six weeks for dinner. It's been that way for more than thirty years.

At a recent dinner with the 88th Street Pussycats, I shared pictures taken of Harry at the graduation party, and the card we had made him. "You know," Cindy said, "seeing that card makes me realize that we were good kids back then and that we thought of someone other than ourselves."

Receiving thanks from Harry twenty-five years later for something we had forgotten we'd done was a true surprise. Reconnecting with a man who was a hero to us because he treated us kindly was a gift. But seeing Harry and the card again through adult eyes, a deeper meaning unveiled itself. He was a safe adult at school, a friendly presence, with no way to influence our report cards; thus he could interact and be available to us in a more relaxed way than our teachers. Given this freedom, Harry chose to build relationships with the students. His smile was an invitation to be his friend.

When people with good intentions sincerely welcome you into their world, they are giving you access to the way in which they live life.

When people with good intentions sincerely welcome you into their world, they are giving you access to the way in which they live life. In Harry's case, he gave four hundred students access to his work. Harry's office was the first time many of us had seen someone's work environment. He built a little community of helpers who felt valued because he made us feel that cleaning erasers was an important first job. In giving of himself, Harry created a bond with us.

At the graduation party, when Harry showed us the card, he revealed again, that our young presence had mattered to him.

Harry turned one hundred in the summer of 2010. A "Happy 100" card made the rounds of the old River Ridge gang to sign it, offering Harry more good wishes.

Colliding into something good from one's past feels serendipitous, as though God pre-orchestrated a lavish delight just for us. When we encounter such a moment, we make a sweet connection between the past and present, and we receive joy.

Something else occurs, too: A BlessBack.

The River Ridge gang recognized Harry's kindness and created a handmade retirement card that specifically said *why* they were thankful. They blessed him back for his kindness, for inviting them into his office, for making the school look good, for coming to their concerts and for learning their names.

Years later, other BlessBacks happened, too. First, when Harry showed Mark the oversized card, he blessed Mark back in two ways. Just revealing that he had kept the twenty-five-year-old card gave Mark a BlessBack, for Harry showed Mark how much he valued the students' recognition. Secondly, Harry told Mark that the kids made just as big an impact on him as he had on them.

Later, when I told the 88th Street Pussycats the story, they received a BlessBack. They learned, as young people, they had unknowingly made a difference in Harry's life, too.

When people give a BlessBack, they are letting another know how he or she impacted their life. When people receive a BlessBack, they discover that they matter and have made a difference in someone's life. When this occurs, a beautiful exchange of blessing — an illumination — happens. BlessBacks, once in motion, are circular, and ever-expanding. The BlessBack of Harry touching our lives, of us touching his life, came around and touched us once again.

> *At times our own light goes out and is*
> *rekindled by a spark from another person.*
> *Each of us has cause to think with deep gratitude*
> *of those who have lighted the flame within us.*

— Albert Schweitzer

Note to Self
Illuminators of Kindness

THE IDEAL – KINDNESS

The ideal the school kids saw in Harry was kindness. He demonstrated this ideal by how he treated the kids, even learning all their names. He showed them his working life and the value he gave to doing a good job, which gave it meaning. Being a janitor, to Harry, meant more than simply maintaining a building. It meant reaching into the children's lives, and doing so in a way and language they understood. When he gave of himself, the children responded back to him in kind.

THE LOOK BACK

Think back to your childhood years. Was there someone who was kind to you? Who was it and how old were you?

How did that person demonstrate kindness to you?

Describe how being around this person made you feel.

As you look back with adult eyes and from some distance in time, is there an underlying reason as to why this person was a point-of-light for you? If so, what do you think it is?

THE INVITATION
How could you, as an illuminator, show kindness as a worthy ideal?

A BLESSBACK COURSE OF ACTION
If your Illuminator of Kindness were sitting with you right now, what three specific things would you say as to how he or she influenced your life?

1.

2.

3.

BENEDICTION

As I begin my BlessBack journey,
may I desire to change,
may I pursue the ideal of kindness as a reason to change.
May I have the courage to change.
And, as I receive the tools to aid me,
may I be empowered to act and thank those people
who illuminated my walk through life in a unique way.

Kindness is the language
which the deaf can hear and the blind can see.

— Mark Twain
Notes From a Traveler Afar

CHAPTER THREE

My BlessBack Journey

Kind words are jewels
that live in the heart and soul,
and remain as blessed memories
years after they have been spoken.

— Marvea Johnson

My BlessBack journey began more than fifteen years ago. I was in a phase where I allowed others to mistreat me. During that miserable time, I had a dream. I was lakeside at a picnic when a friend made an unkind comment about me. She laughed in front of my peers when she saw her dart had wounded. In silence, I fled and went to start my boat at the dock. Three women in dresses, gloves, veiled hats, and holding purses walked to me. One, with mother-of-pearl inlays on her glasses, pursed her lips, and angled her head as she stared me down. "Do you speak when you have something to say?" she said. I had started the engine but, frozen by her statement, could not shift it into reverse.

I jolted upright in bed, away from her haunting words, but they did not stop chasing me.

I grew up in a close-knit home with my mom, dad and two brothers. The summer lights of Met Stadium lit my bedroom on evenings the Minnesota Twins had games. I fell asleep serenaded by the crowd's roar when Killebrew homered or Carew stole second base. In my mind, I was with the fans too, cheering from a wooden bleacher, digging my wooden stick into a Frosty Malt.

Auntie Mame said in the movie *Mame* that "Life is a banquet and I've never been one to miss out on its courses." When I am around people,

I don't feel like I'm missing out. I love to be around them, to watch how they interact and to listen to their stories. My father always said, "Who's more fun than people?" People energize me and their energy is contagious. They want to be a part of something bigger than themselves. They want to contribute. The more I observe them, the more I see how much they play a part in the story of the world as it is being lived out now.

But somewhere along the path of listening, I began to allow negative people to influence me. Instead of creating a personal boundary of respect, I let their words in and they seared. The attacks became personal and I listened when cut down.

Soon I became afraid to express my point of view. I worried that whatever I said was wrong and would evoke an attack, so I said nothing. I became depressed and backed away from life. My being changed places with my shadow.

Most of us have dark moments at some time or another. The sixteenth century Spanish mystic St. John of the Cross called those times *la noche oscura del alma*: the dark night of the soul. Somehow I needed to climb from the darkness and find my purpose. I needed to find me again.

Not long after my dream, Sue, one of the 88th Street Pussycats, took me to lunch. She spoke from her heart as well as on behalf of the others. "We're concerned and worried about you," she said. "You used to laugh at your own jokes, sometimes until you cried. Now you hardly talk at dinner and sometimes you don't even come. It feels like you've taken yourself out of life. We're wondering where the old Julie has gone."

I told her I felt like I had tucked the true me inside. "I'm worried I'll say the wrong thing."

"So what if you say the wrong thing?" Sue said. "I'm always saying things I have to apologize for later. No one's perfect. It's okay to be you. The old Julie was great the way she was. She didn't need to change. It's time for her to come out and play again."

Listening is a magnetic and strange thing, a creative force.
The friends who listen to us are the ones we move toward.
When we are listened to, it creates us, makes us unfold and expand.

— Karl A. Menninger

That day was a wake-up call. For too long I had allowed people who were not my friends to exert their influence over me to the point of silencing me. I wanted to jump the track and ride life's rails again. I started in the most trustworthy place I knew.

I read the Bible, wrote my reflections in my journal and made some discoveries. My watershed came in looking at my life in comparison to the Apostle Paul's. Prior to his conversion to Christianity, Paul was en route to arrest members of an offshoot of Judaism when Jesus struck him blind for three days. Paul was never blind to faith again. Jailed, flogged, stoned, ridiculed, arrested, and nearly killed, Paul still spoke his mind wherever he went. Where did Paul get that kind of audacity to speak?

A relationship with Jesus became the plinth of his faith. Paul's heart, emboldened by Jesus and filled with a passion for people, changed our world.

Secondly, angels and dreams gave Paul courage. Angels visited him in jail and directed his words and actions. Many times his dreams gave him the next course on his journey and, with those directions, the confidence to do so.

Third, he used his knowledge to empower him. Paul was fluent in Hebrew, Arabic, Greek and Latin. As both a Pharisee and a Roman citizen, he knew Jewish and Roman laws. His credentials went before him and gave him authority to speak.

He also loved people and kept in contact with them after he left an area. Companions and friends told him about the newly formed churches; these oral reports encouraged him. He received letters from the churches he had left behind. Their written words helped him continue his mission. In response, Paul wrote the churches and fondly expressed his memories of their time together. He went around the world "doing good," despite times of persecution.

Looking at Paul's life gave me a fresh way to look at mine. Here's what I found:

Jesus lived in me, too. I asked Him to get me back on track and for courage to do so. James' words are true: "Draw near to God and He will draw near to you." I started reading the Bible, sometimes self-directed, other times using guides, and God's presence came near.

I went to visit my cousin Jacki Beaulieu in Phoenix. That spring was a particularly rainy one. As we rode quietly on horseback in a desert preserve filled with flowering cacti, words from a song whispered in my mind, "The desert of the heart can be transformed if you open your heart to the Lord." And it did. Messages about the desert's ability to bloom seemed everywhere, on the news, in books, and on the radio. A devotional held a verse from Jeremiah: "A path through the waters will be suddenly opened." God was speaking to my heart. He was at work restoring me.

And, like Paul, I had had a life-changing dream. The words from the woman with mother-of-pearl glasses had burrowed into me for a reason: I could be useful in this world by giving of myself, whether it was expressing my opinion or sharing my experience.

Lastly, like Paul, I had a backstory. Different from Paul's but similar in that I was here in this place and time for a reason. I began to explore my life and the people who had passed through, asking myself why they had made an indelible connection with my spirit.

A COMMON DAY

I keep a Box of Common Days. I don't know where the name came from to describe an ordinary shoebox stored on a bedroom closet shelf. One day when I was blue, I went to my closet. Letters, postcards, and thank-you notes made the sides of the box bulge. I brought it down and realized I was holding a log book of voyages. Thirty-four years of people sharing themselves filled that box. I sat on my closet floor and time spilled out. Postcards from France, Japan, Korea, Italy, and many states held people's travel memories. I opened letters from friends, the stationery unique to the person. Their words put helium into my soul:

I began to explore my life and the people who had passed through, asking myself why they had made an indelible connection with my spirit.

Striped airmail letters from a friend when she cared for children in Cameroon. A postcard from someone in Oregon with whom I had lost contact. Notes from my friend Debbie, written in bright blue ink. Another, a note filled with heart-shaped i's written by a girl in a children's choir I once directed. Another from a goddaughter, her envelope filled with glittery stickers. I think the oldest note was from my cousin Karen, then nine, who wrote how much she enjoyed my family visiting hers in Sun Prairie, Wisconsin. Her penciled words in hills and valleys showed she was hard at work on her cursive letters. I read another, this one from former Prime Minister Tony Blair of 10 Downing Street, thanking me for taking the time to write my thanks for his loving tribute to Princess Diana. Beneath the letters lay an old autograph book from my elementary years. I found Mr. Porter's page, thanking me for bringing a cow's heart to our fourth grade class so we could dissect it. I picked up a thick envelope, letters of the history of my brother and sister-in-law from 1986 when they spent Steve's pastoral internship in Colombia, South America.

My box is anything but common. It is tactile evidence of a lived life. Ruminating in my good memories helped me find my old self. With each immersion into the surround sound of my past, I resurfaced.

The contents imparted something else: the residual effects of being thanked. When I finished my look back through letters, my mental outlook had changed. No longer did I feel devalued. My attitude became positive. My past had, letter by letter, pushed me into the game of life, not only to stay but to thrive: Rereading the notes made me want to do something to pass my thank-full feelings along. I wanted to write letters of gratitude, which I came to think of as BlessBacks.

Still feeling a bit tentative, I started offering BlessBacks to those who were the farthest and safest points out: people who had had an effect on me but whom I didn't know personally. I came across a short saying in late 1999 by Marion Wright Edelman. I think it is lovely still:

Learn to be quiet enough to hear the
sound of the genuine
within yourself
so that you can hear it in others.[1]

Finding the author's address took some time and led me to the Children's Defense Fund organization she had founded. Touched by Ms. Edelman's expressed beauty, I sent her a note so that she would know it. Writing her that letter felt as though I was sending good into the world.

I received a small envelope in January 2000. The imprinted return address was a light blue sailboat; beneath it was child-like scrawling that said,

"Dear Lord. Be good to me. The sea is so wide and my boat is so small." Inside was a letter of two lines.

> *Thank you for your kind and encouraging letter.*
> *I'm grateful that* Guide My Feet *has helped you.*
> *A blessed new year to you.*
>   *Sincerely yours,*
>   *Marian Wright Edelman*

And so I embarked from my still life in the harbor of silence and set course to thank those people in it who provided me a compass. Some small and some deeply meaningful and personal to me, my BlessBacks continue to change, empower and reshape my life. Living the BlessBack life, to quote what Hemingway said about Paris, has become a movable feast. The practice goes wherever I go. I journey with intention to a place called Change and on a weekly basis I give a BlessBack, whether in person, on the phone or by a letter.

As a result, I love life again. I invite the bespectacled woman by the lake in my dreams to ask me again, "Do you speak when you have something to say?" I have a wonderful, transformative answer for her now.

EMERGENT COASTLINES

Tectonic plates bump and drift under the ocean and disrupt coastlines a few centimeters each year. Submergent coastlines, such as Norway's fjords and the Chesapeake Bay estuary, occur when land sinks relative to the area's rising sea level. Conversely, emergent coastlines, like Belize's coral reef, are created when land rises, comparatively speaking, to the area's sea level.[2]

Humans too, are not static. Inside and out, we are in constant motion. Gravity tugs. Our skin weathers and wrinkles; our joints wear.

In our brains lies the limbic system, which allows us to emote, learn and remember. Philosopher Martha Nussbaum said emotions are "intelligent responses to the perception of value."[3] We react or respond emotionally to what or with whom we interact. It's in our nature.

A coral reef is an example of an emergent coastline. Because the reef is above sea level, it acts as a barrier against waves and thus protects the thriving sea life on its other side. Stephen Marshak, head of the geology department at the University of Illinois, Urbana-Champaign, writes, "Reefs ... serve as a living buffer zone that protects coasts from erosion."[4]

When my family visited Caye Caulker, Belize, we snorkeled and swam over the reef. The buffer zone of the reef protected against crushing waves. A thriving, safe, healthy environment existed there. Underwater, the sea was full of the sun's light. The variety of life, shapes, and forms — sea anemones, sponges, multi-colored iridescent fish — even the corals' texture had beauty. Their colors were brilliant, vibrant, healthy. The water was calm and free of turmoil. Long after you left its sanctuary, the sensation of peace, the memory of safety, stayed with you.

Just as there are people whose hurtful words hinder, impede and cause us to hide our true selves, there are people — parents, friends, strangers, neighbors, coaches, teachers or siblings —who provide wave- and windbreaks and act as illuminators. They build us up with encouraging words, blessings, or acts of kindness. Just as coral reefs shield a coastline from erosion, these good people help us to emerge and flourish. They protect us, mentally and emotionally. We allow them to gatekeep our hearts because we trust them not to hurt us. We want to be around them; we feel oxygenated by them. "The playground of freedom is love," said W. A. Sadler, and in the presence of positive influencers, we are free. We can be ourselves, play and be loved.

Love in this way produces real geological upheavals of thought.

— Marcel Proust

Housed in Dickens' pages is one of literature's finest characters: Joe Gargery in *Great Expectations*. Joe is the perfect example of an illuminator. He views people with one lens: he sees the good they do. He hears people with only one ear: the one in which he hears the good things people have to say. His response to everything in life is to say,

"Astonishing. As-TON-ishing!"[5] He truly believes every person he meets is the best thing that could happen to him all day.

If a realistic person were to look at Joe's life, that person would say that he has a crummy life. He lives in an abusive situation. His wife physically beats him every day. He is illiterate. He is poor and to mix up the menu eats broth one day and bread the next. He is a blacksmith, where life is mundane and spent alone near hot coals.

But Joe lives life as though his circumstances were invisible to him. Every new minute Joe sees as a fresh and bright new possibility he can use to be joy-filled. Each new second holds something that can and *will* astonish him. He asks of the day, "Astonish me!" and the day does.

My husband and I have a friend who lives life like Joe does. His name is Rick Lindblom. If you ask him, "How are you?" Rick's response is always the same. "If I were any happier, I'd have to be two people."

That same astonishing and joy-filled feeling comes when we encounter those whose acts or words encourage, enrich or equip us for our future, or even for the day. These upheavals uplift, propel and sustain. Our souls put out the welcome mat and we keep their words close to our hearts. Our life influencers are our barrier reefs, living buffers against the storms, seen or unforeseen, small or significant. They make life's negative moments bearable and remind us to play.

Our life influencers are our barrier reefs, living buffers against the storms, seen or unforeseen, small or significant.

Have you heard a song or smelled a scent and it triggered a memory of someone who understood you, who loved you? The memory pulls us from the moment and we inhale and pause. We see and hear that person's voice of courage, championing us to become the person we hope we can become. How they were, how their words lifted us when we doubted ourselves, is an upheaval of the best kind. Their significance empowers and gives us energy.

When we look back to those who positively influenced us, our insecurities and fears vanish. No shade darkens our memory's landscape because the positive memories bring sweetness and light. They are upheavals of goodness. They trump our fears. They grant us permission to walk into the gateway of our future. Cloaked in the memory of their words, we are able, as Eleanor Roosevelt said, "to do the thing we think we cannot do."

One of life's greatest gifts is retracing our lives. Robert Louis Stevenson called this reflection "the only end of life." We learn we mattered to someone. A BlessBack takes us out of an ordinary day, an ordinary life. The cobwebs disappear, revealing a beautiful memory.

Something else happens, too. We are given a gift. Someone was paying attention to our words or actions. The BlessBack becomes an expression of our worth — not in a prideful or self-appreciative way, but in a fulfilled way. We, a work-in-progress, see our progress.

Life shrinks or expands in proportion to one's courage.

— Anaïs Nin

THE IDEAL – COURAGE

My dream was the catalyst I needed to start believing in myself again, but courage didn't come overnight. What unleashed me was:

a realization that I needed to change

a desire to change

a conversation with God and a trusted friend

surveying the landscape of my past and looking for the positive people there who spoke truth to me

Courage as an ideal requires a conviction to pursue what you believe in. When you come out the other side, you'll look back and see the gained ground and say, "I have something important to give to the world because of the trip."

THE LOOK BACK

In your journey through life so far, who are the people who have been like a coral reef to you, those who, while in their company, make you feel safe from the waves and winds of life? Who allows you to be yourself when you are around them?

Courage is gained in steps. Sometimes those steps are inches long, other times the step might take you off a cliff and into waters below. For the times you've taken a courageous step, from where or from whom did you receive the courage to make a positive change in your life?

Who has shown courage to you by speaking the kind of truth that hurts or stings but turned out to be what you needed to hear?

What was the inciting incident?

What did your Captain Courageous say that allowed you to look at yourself honestly?

How is your life different or better because his or her words or actions spoke truth into your life?

THE INVITATION

If you have personally experienced someone's act of courage toward you, then you know that person risked his relationship with you to do so. He forged ahead and spoke truth into your life because the person cared more about your character than whether the conversation was comfortable or not. Is there someone today who needs to see you being gently courageous before he or she can be? If so, write the person's name and think of how you can tread softly and show that courage is a worthy ideal.

A BLESSBACK COURSE OF ACTION

Even captains in courage appreciate being thanked. How could you give a BlessBack to them and what reasons would you give as to why you are thankful they modeled this ideal to you?

BENEDICTION

As I revisit my life,
I'm becoming aware how much of it required courage.
As I go forward in my BlessBack journey,
give me the courage to step out or speak up and give a BlessBack.
For I know if I do,
I will have an opportunity to make a difference in someone's life.

Don't be surprised as you travel,
if in the process, someone brings Change to you.

Notes From a Traveler Afar

PART TWO

Why a BlessBack
is Beneficial

CHAPTER FOUR

Building a Better You

A place where happiness never melts.

— Swensen's Ice Cream Parlors' slogan

Through the years, the advertising industry in the West has tried to convince us happiness is tied to what we wear, how we wear it, and that we own stylish homes and expensive vehicles in which to move and live with our happy selves.

Over the span of the past forty years, the field of positive psychology and their thousands of empirical studies is proving happiness doesn't come to us this way. Instead, once our basic needs are met, studies show what makes us mentally and physically happier has to do with giving to others. Intentionally performing acts of kindness for strangers as well as for those we care most about leads to a gratitude-filled life. In other words, it takes effort to be happy, and that effort isn't about money or material possessions — it's about people.

BLESSBACK, THE HAPPINESS TONIC

German physicist and writer Stefan Klein wrote in *The Science of Happiness* that brain scientists can now observe the brain as it thinks and feels. "They can see how joy arises in our brain when we think of someone we love."[1]

Klein writes that our brains "have a special circuitry for joy, pleasure, and euphoria – we have a happiness system. Just as we come into the world with a capacity for speech, we are also programmed for positive feelings.[2] A still more surprising discovery is that the adult brain continues to change; the circuits in our brain are altered whenever we learn something, and new connections are forged in our network of nerve cells. [T]hese changes are triggered by thoughts, but even more by emotions. This means that with the right exercises we can increase our capacity for happiness."[3]

Psychologist Sonja Lyubomirsky's $1 million, five-year grant from the National Institute of Mental Health has enabled her to investigate whether happiness can last.[4] Armed with the 1970s study that lottery winners quickly returned a year later to their former happiness levels, Lyubomirsky developed a Subjective Happiness Scale with crosschecks to ensure for accurate data. Using kindness, gratitude, and optimism as her rubrics, she and her colleagues discovered that fifty percent of our happiness is genetic. We can't change our genes. Ten percent of our happiness is circumstantial, which we also cannot control. But we can control an astonishing forty percent of our happiness levels by doing intentional activities that are positive.[5] Lyubomirsky concluded that being aware of our blessings, showing gratitude, and doing acts of kindness all elevate happiness.

Here's a brief rundown of a few of Lyubomirsky's findings:[6]

1. To be successful in sustaining happiness, the participants have to be intentional with "cognitive, behavioral, and goal-based activities" that focus on keeping their happiness levels up.
2. Those who attained "happiness sustainability" did so when they found reasons to stay motivated to increase their happiness levels.
3. People who were proactive in sustaining their happiness levels practiced kindness five times a day. These included simple acts like opening the door for a stranger, taking a neighbor's trash out, or doing their roommates' dishes. These participants increased their happiness levels, whereas those in the no-treatment group did not.
4. Repeating the same acts of kindness resulted in little change in participants' happiness levels. Activities became routine and ineffective. Only when participants mixed up their types of acts of kindness did they boost their happiness to higher levels.

"Grateful thinking promotes the savoring of positive life experiences," Lyubomirsky said at Gratefulness.org. "By relishing and taking pleasure in some of the gifts of your life, you will be able to extract maximum possible satisfaction and enjoyment from your current circumstances." Lyubomirsky also found participants had greater success with sustained happiness if they practiced gratitude once a week.[7]

"Gratitude is the antidote to negative emotions," said Lyubomirsky in a January 2008 article in Britain's *Sunday Express*. "[It is a] neutralizer of envy, avarice, worry and hostility."[8]

You cannot be depressed and grateful at the same time. The states are counter-intuitive to each other. By using positive thoughts, implementing acts of kindness and BlessBacks, you really can "train your brain" and live a happier life.

By using positive thoughts, implementing acts of kindness and BlessBacks, you really can "train your brain" and live a happier life.

To change your language you must change your life.

— Derek Walcott

THE POWER IN REMINISCENCE

Katie Lizeth was in her junior year at college and working towards her elementary education degree. She was in the throes of finals. For one final, she had to create twenty-two daily lesson plans. Each one had to include English, physical education, art, science and math and the lessons had to be adaptable to students in the English-as-a-Second-Language program. To divert feelings of stress and being overwhelmed, Katie and her roommate decided to look at her freshman year photo album and old wall posts on Facebook. Doing so did two things for Katie. "We looked at them to take a break from doing some hard work," she said. "But also, looking at those albums and posts made me remember my new life that started here at college. Just by talking about the good memories I had from being here made me realize all the good things I had done and how far I had come."

A study conducted at Loyola University of Chicago in 2005 found college students used the recollection of memories to enhance their lives and to help them transition to living in a campus environment. Fred Bryant and his group of psychologists conducted their experiment with 1,280 students at two Midwestern private colleges as part of a college psychology course requirement. They also looked to see if college students and older adults who practiced reminiscing shared any commonality, using the early discoveries of their peers to build on their hypotheses.[9] They are listed here:

- Reminiscing helped older adults bolster their identities when they looked back at their positive past and saw that it was unique.[10]
- Reminiscing increased older adults' self-esteem when they remembered their positive past and savored it for the simple enjoyment it brought in doing so.[11]
- Reminiscing helped older adults cope with stress and their current physical situation when they escaped into the positive memories of their past.[12]
- Reminiscing helped older adults transition and adjust to new environments, whether it was moving to a retirement home or encountering changes to their bodies. Doing so gave them comfort and helped them with conflict resolution in their present situation.[13]

Bryant discovered that both the aged population and college students shared similar results when they positively reminisced. Their reasons:

- **Doing so helped them feel good about themselves today.** One young woman said that looking into her past for positive memories "gave me an idea of where I was then, where I am now, and where I ultimately want to be," she wrote. "These memories also give me a sense of confidence, kind of a 'you did it before, you can do it again' type of thing."[14]

"Consistent with research using elderly samples," wrote Bryant et al., "the more time that college students reported reminiscing about pleasant memories, the more they felt able to enjoy their lives."[15]

- **Doing so helped them adapt to their new environment.** Students reminisced to help them shift from home life to campus life just as older adults did to help themselves with their changing environments. Bryant's study found reminiscing helps a person to adapt by way of "increasing awareness and providing a sense of perspective in the present."[16]
- **Both students and seniors used mementos and souvenirs to aid in their positive reminiscing.** Both age groups used tools of their era such as bulletin boards, shadow boxes, Facebook, scrapbooks, saved letters, photographs and listening to music, to remember the good things in their past.[17]

Many nursing homes have shadow boxes outside residents' rooms filled with wedding and family pictures, tickets, baseball cards, playbills and sheet music – mementos of bygone times. Ann Seymour worked as community relations communicator at a senior assisted-living home. "We had a wing there called 'Reminiscence,'" she said, "designed to help bring positive memories of times past to the residents and to keep positive reminders around them of loved ones and happy times. A large highboy with a dozen or so pull-out drawers stored memorabilia from bygone eras to help residents remember those times and for visitors to use in conversations with our residents."

Alma Otto made the adjustment from living independently in an apartment in a small Wisconsin town to moving to an assisted-living complex two hours away in Minneapolis because of encouraging letters she received from folks "back home." She saved each letter and reread them countless times. She loved to hear how her friends were doing. She felt as if she were still a part of their lives even though they no longer drove and could not visit her in the nursing home. The more letters she received, the more they helped her to realize that in the same way she made friends long ago, she could make friends in her new home. The letters helped her transition to her new living arrangement.

Walt Whitman called remembering "a backward glance o'er travell'd roads." Visiting long-ago memories not only aids us in keeping our self-worth and remembering some good times, but it also reveals the valued people in our past, how we built and sustained friendships, and the histories we share with them.

> Visiting long-ago memories... reveals the valued people in our past, how we built and sustained friendships, and the histories we share with them.

GET HEALTHY, BLESSBACK

Worry, stress, and anxiety are words of the times in which we live, but by giving BlessBacks, we can actually change our physical well-being. Since 1991, Doc Childre, founder of the Institute of HeartMath, a nonprofit research and educational organization, has promoted the connections between the heart and the brain and found ways for people to live healthier and stress-free. One of his methods is appreciation.[18] *The HeartMath Solution*, is written by Childre, Howard Martin and Donna Beech. In it, the authors explain effective ways to manage stress as well as the benefits to using our hearts to do so. The authors explain that our physical hearts have intelligence.

When we shift our focus to our hearts along with thinking about something for which we are appreciative, we can bring our mental states and our body systems under control. When we achieve that control, our heart rates slow down, our blood pressures decrease, our respirations come under control, our brains are fed more oxygen and we will feel calmer and can think more clearly.[19]

Childre developed two processes. The first, called FREEZE-FRAME, is a calming method for highly-stressed clients. They shift from concentrating on their stress to focusing on their physical heart. They are encouraged to imagine for at least ten seconds that they are breathing through their heart and as they do, to think about a happy time in their life, whether it was an incident or a person, and to re-create the memory in their mind. Next, the clients acknowledge their stress but then form a common-sense response to that stress. Childre encourages his clients to practice FREEZE-FRAME daily.[20]

When Patricia came to HeartMath, her heart was beating seven hundred additional beats per hour. Over the course of a weekend of practicing the FREEZE-FRAME process, her heart rate returned to normal. Patricia now incorporates the FREEZE-FRAME process into each day.[21]

In another study, eight weeks after implementing the technique, participants, without any other change in habits, had significantly lowered their blood pressure. Sixty-five percent felt calmer and eighty-seven percent reported being less tired.[22]

Five hundred staff members at Delnor Community Hospital in Chicago went through HeartMath's training. Results include decreased staff turnovers; in addition, patient stays decreased while patient care satisfaction increased.[23]

Childre's second process, to be practiced for five to fifteen minutes, is the Heart Lock-In. With this method, clients use the FREEZE-FRAME method, but as they focus on imagining breathing through their heart, they also focus on "feeling appreciation for someone or something in [their lives]. As a result, participants' health improved, especially when they used gratitude as a way to shift their stress-filled thoughts.[24]

Childre's lab results showed that when patients concentrated on the heart, breathing in and out, and focusing on the love they feel for a specific person in their lives and their gratefulness for that individual, the patients brought their bodies' systems under control. When a person worked to experience what Childre calls "core heart feelings," that person provided "regeneration to the nervous system, the immune system, and the hormonal system, facilitating health and well-being." The important factor that made the process most effective was "to reexperience the feeling [of gratefulness]."[25]

By focusing on both our heart and our gratitude, we change our heart rate and blood pressure. Childre's patients are proving that living a gratitude-filled life can improve our physical well-being. The better we feel, the better we function.

Practicing Childre's techniques can change a person's life; the hard part is to create the habit. Bruce Cryer, HeartMath's global director, believes we can permanently improve mental and physical health in ourselves with practice. He likens living every day using the HeartMath techniques to that of other daily activities. "Every day I get dressed. I don't occasionally get dressed," he said in *T & D* magazine. "Every day, I eat. I don't occasionally eat." Cryer has created a daily ritual with HeartMath concepts that are as natural to him as living and breathing.[26]

In another study, multiple sclerosis patients shown an altruistic film about Mother Teresa experienced a rise in immune efficiency. After the film, selected participants were asked to remember when they felt most loved in their own lives. Doing so boosted their immune system and its effects lasted another hour.[27]

According to Ronald Glaser, a virologist at Ohio State, "stressed-out grumblers are two-and-half times more susceptible to colds than grateful people."[28]

Giving or receiving a BlessBack acts as a tonic to our soul.

In California, Hispanic students who agreed to participate in a study found their test anxiety decreased prior to being tested when they were shown an altruistic act on a computer screen.[29]

We have much to learn about the correlation between practicing gratitude and how it relates to our physical bodies, but these studies reveal that gratitude plays a positive role in our well-being. Gratefulness is an elixir for good mental and physical health. Giving or receiving a BlessBack acts as a tonic to our soul.

We are not permitted to choose the frame of our destiny.
But what we put into it is ours.

— Dag Hammarskjöld

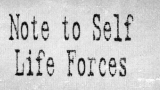

THE IDEAL – LIFE FORCES

Newton's first law of motion is this: An object at rest tends to stay at rest until a force causes the object to move. Applied to this chapter's point, we have discovered that forty percent of our happiness levels are malleable, but to increase those levels, we have to interrupt our status quo, practice, and train our brain.

The same principle applies to another aspect of this law: An object in motion stays in motion until it encounters another force. By using Doc Childre's FREEZE-FRAME or Heart Lock-In methods, we can halt the speed and levels of our stress and bring ourselves into healthier states simply by thinking about someone we appreciate.

Working with these laws of physics in our own situations can only happen if we let these life forces ignite us into action.

THE LOOK BACK

A Quaker woman used to sit quietly for two hours each day. She called the time her "still lessons." Put yourself into a quiet place, right where you are. Concentrate on your heart and still your worries. Close your eyes and take five cleansing breaths, in through your nose, slowly exhaling through your mouth. Now, think about a happy time in your life, one for which you feel grateful. Write down the time in your life and the people in it.

What emotions in the memory do you feel?

How does your body feel after doing this exercise?

THE INVITATION

Our heart is a pump, but even this muscle rests between beats. It uses that time to fill up with blood so at the next beat it is equipped to send its life force where it needs to go. You, too, have the choice each day to fill up your tank; methods like BlessBacks can help you recharge. Habits take thirty-seven days to create. Where in your days this week will you make time to BlessBack, using the still lessons taught in this chapter?

A BLESSBACK COURSE OF ACTION

By using your body's own life forces, along with gratitude, you can exercise control if you use the empowering tools in this chapter. If the people you've thought about are appropriate for you to contact, find their names and addresses and write them below.

As you practice these lifestyle changes, write a list of people you appreciate as you go through the book and practice the skills learned in this chapter each day of this week.

BENEDICTION

I feel empowered now,
knowing that by using gratitude, my body, mind, and my heart,
I can change my life.
I do want to change
and believe using life forces with gratitude
is an ideal truly worthy of my pursuit.
Today I will still myself and listen to the whispered lessons found there
as I create this new habit of living a happier, grateful life.

*There shall be
eternal summer in the grateful heart.*

— Celia Thaxter
Notes From a Traveler Afar

CHAPTER FIVE
Building Up and Blessing Others

Let me live in a house by the side of the road
and be a friend to man.

— Sam Walter Foss

As we've seen in the previous chapter, connecting with another person by giving a BlessBack will make you healthier, but validating another person's purpose and acknowledging his or her existence will also inspire and satisfy you both. It will build up the receivers of your BlessBack so that they are empowered to give BlessBacks of their own. The ripple effect of BlessBacks is that they have the potential to make a world of difference.

FINDING NORMAL

Gloria Plaisted and her husband attend annual conferences to keep abreast of industry trends and forecasts in the restaurant franchise business. Their trip to Florida in November 2007 was no exception. The morning of the first day of the conference, they stood in line outside their hotel to take a shuttle bus to Orlando's convention center, ready for an agenda-filled day.

They climbed the bus stairs. Single seats remained. Gloria sat next to a woman and, seeing her name tag, smiled. "You're from Faulkton, South Dakota?" she said. "You don't happen to know a Sheriff Wherry, do you?"

"I do," the woman said. "My husband was state attorney and he and Sheriff Wherry worked together many times before the sheriff retired."

"I used to know Sheriff Wherry, too," Gloria said as the bus arrived at the conference. "I'll never forget him."

Thirteen months later, back home in Minnesota, Gloria was on her way to Duluth when suddenly she felt the urge to contact Sheriff Wherry. She pulled to the shoulder and dialed 411. As the operator located Sheriff Wherry's number, Gloria's mind tripped back to the 1960s.

Flower power, psychedelic rock, and drugs. April 1968 was the height of hippie culture and opposition to the Vietnam War. Gloria's home life was turbulent, too. Her mother had died of cancer seven years before, when Gloria was eight. Since then, her brother and sister had gone to live in foster homes. But Gloria was stuck living in a home in the ghettos of St. Paul with a father who, it seemed to her, did not care about her. She felt the only reason her father kept her at home was to keep the Social Security and welfare checks coming so he could feed his gambling habit. And he paid even less attention to her once he married his new wife, Katherine. Gloria's only comfort was the love of Rick, her eighteen-year-old boyfriend. He wanted to escape, too. He was tired of living in a YMCA and eating twelve-cent hamburgers and malted milk balls purchased with found coins.

Two months shy of finishing her sophomore year, she pleaded with her father to allow her to live with her half-sister, Sandy and her family, in California. After she ran away twice, her father agreed to let her go. Rick promised to move with her.

Gloria arrived first by bus and finished out the remainder of the school year. Rick and his friend Mike followed after their high school graduations in June.

Two weeks into their new life, reality hit. Rick couldn't find a job and the couple's little cash had dwindled to a few dollars. Life at Gloria's sister's home was not working, either. Sandy objected to Gloria and Rick spending so much time alone. Sandy pulled the welcome mat July 1, forcing Gloria to phone home. Katherine answered and asked to speak to Rick.

"She wants me to bring you home," Rick said, hanging up. "But I won't if you don't want me to."

"I don't want to go back there," Gloria said, "but it's our only option."

The following night, the young couple helped Mary, Gloria's friend, to babysit. After putting the children to bed, Gloria walked into the living room, with Mary following her. Rick had his jacket on.

"C'mon, let's go, Gloria. I want to leave for home tonight," he said. "We can drive through the night without much traffic."

Rick's eyes seemed different to Gloria. He wouldn't look directly at her. "Why are you all of a sudden in a hurry?" she said. "We don't have our stuff with us. Besides, don't we have about ten dollars to our name?"

"You don't need to worry about that," he said.

"How are we going to get home?" Gloria said.

"Mike's Mustang. He won't care if we borrow it." Rick twirled her blond ponytail and pulled her to him. "I've got everything under control, Gloria. Let's go."

Mary reached into her purse. "You can't drive all that way without any money," she said. "Here's forty dollars at least."

Gloria thanked her friend and they said their hasty good-byes. Gloria had always trusted Rick's judgment. This time was no different. Snuggling under his arm in the ragtop, she tried not to let her mind get ahead of each mile. But as the sun set over the Pacific, the lovebirds were running from more than their family problems. Unknown to them, they were running from something new this time: the law.

The clutch went out in the middle of South Dakota. A car filled with teenagers came by and offered them a ride into the town of Faulkton, a few miles away. The owner of the town's only service station towed the Mustang to his garage. He told them it wouldn't be ready until noon the next day.

A motel across the street flashed a neon "vacancy" and Gloria waited outside while Rick rented a room. On Main Street, they found a café and ordered a hamburger to split. Gloria wolfed her half down. They hadn't eaten in forty-eight hours. She swallowed her last bite but noticed Rick's half was still on his plate. "What's wrong?" she said.

He fingered a fork and shrugged.

"Fine. Don't tell me," Gloria said. She slid out of the booth to call her stepmother from a phone outside to let her know where they were.

"Your sister is really mad that you two just took off without letting her know. She's put out an arrest warrant on Rick," Gloria heard her stepmother say as the town's sheriff walked into the restaurant. Gloria tried not to panic, told Katherine they'd be home soon and walked back into the restaurant.

Seated at the counter, the sheriff drank from his coffee cup. He was a strapping man who looked like Sheriff Andy Taylor from *The Andy Griffith Show* on TV.

"Rick," she whispered as she slid into the booth, "There is a warrant

out for you — supposedly because you took me across state lines."
There was sweat on his forehead and he was rubbing his hands together.
"What's the matter? You look so nervous."

"When we were with Mary babysitting, I took a checkbook lying on
the counter at the Adams' house," he said.

Gloria looked at the sheriff then back to Rick. "Are you serious?" She
blinked back tears and felt the room close in around her.

"Don't look at me like that, Gloria," he said, keeping his voice low.

"Is that how you paid for our motel room?"

He cocked a repentant smirk. "I was out of ideas. I think the sheriff
might be here looking for us. We gotta turn ourselves in."

As the sheriff left the café, Rick took Gloria's hand and they followed
the sheriff outside. "Hello, sir?" he said to the sheriff. "I'd like to talk to
you."

The sheriff turned and looked at them. "Sure, son, what's on your
mind?"

Rick explained their situation, then said, "I think you probably know
I wrote a bad check this afternoon to pay for a motel room. I wasn't
planning to, but our car broke down three miles back and we were
stranded. We haven't stopped driving since leaving California two days
ago. I had to find us a safe place to stay tonight while the car gets fixed."

"I see," the sheriff said. "How old are you two?"

Rick gave their ages.

"I'm sorry to have to do this to you, kids, but I'm going to have to
bring you in."

At the county jail, mug shots were taken. Rick called his parents;
Gloria called her stepmother again. They repeated their story to the
sheriff and gave him their contact information.

An hour passed before the sheriff returned. "In talking with your
family members and law enforcement in California, I've learned there
is not a warrant for you, Rick," Sheriff said. "Your sister told your
stepmother that to scare you both for running off without telling
anyone. There would have been a charge against you because you took
an underage girl across state lines, but I've clarified with Katherine you
were acting as Gloria's guardian and she gave you permission to bring
her home. Now, let's talk about the '68 Mustang. Is it yours?"

"No, sir. It's my friend Mike's car. I had permission to use it. I just didn't tell him I was going to Minnesota with it."

"I see. Well, as far as the law is concerned, you can't be charged with stealing a car as you had your friend's permission to use and drive it. There are no charges on you. Except for one thing." He opened his drawer and set the forged check Rick had written down onto his blotter. "What are we going to do about this?"

"I'm willing to do anything. I will pay it back, sir."

Sheriff Wherry said, "It's a little deeper and more complicated than that, Rick. Is your name Patty Adams?"

"No, sir."

"See Rick, you signed the wrong name and that means you now have a forgery charge against you."

"A forgery charge? I didn't know that writing a bad check was considered forgery, sir."

The sheriff leaned back in his chair. "You both seem like you are good kids who made some errors in judgment," he said. "Unfortunately, you're going to have to spend the night in jail until arrangements can be made for the judge to see you tomorrow."

Alone in the female cell in the basement, Gloria was spooked by the silence. All the years of her father leaving her at night while he gambled, all the evenings she spent walking sidewalks, looking in the windows of neighboring homes hoping a family would ask her in for supper, had created a girl who hated to be alone. She banged on the radiator, stopping only to make sure they heard her wailing. "I'm scared. Please, Sheriff. I promise I'll be good. Please come, please. I'm so afraid!"

Thirty minutes later, the sheriff moved her next to Rick's cell. At dinner time, a woman walked in carrying three plates on a platter. A little boy and girl each carried a plate. The sheriff gave the woman a quick kiss, put his arm around her shoulders, and smiled. "Thanks, honey. This looks wonderful. Hi, kids. This is Gloria and this is Rick. They're going to be with us for a few days. As you can see," he said to Gloria and Rick, "this is a small operation. My wife Marion and I and our three children live in an apartment downstairs."

Gloria removed the aluminum foil and inhaled the hot homemade fried chicken, mashed potatoes, biscuits, and gravy. She dabbed a forkful of potatoes into the gravy and swallowed. "This is so good. Thank you, ma'am."

Marion nodded. "I'm glad you liked it. You'll be seeing me a lot. I'm the one who will make sure you get three square meals a day."

Three meals a day, Gloria thought, *I'll eat better in jail than I ever have in my life.*

Later that night, they lay in their cells. "I know we're in jail, Rick, but I feel safe here," Gloria said.

"I know what you mean, Gloria. The Wherrys, they're like nothing we've ever seen."

"Does this kind of life exist, where a mom and dad love each other? He even kissed her. Did you see how he treated his kids? It's like we're in Mayberry."

The next afternoon the district attorney came with bad news. The judge had left on a two-week fishing trip before ruling on their case and couldn't be reached. Sheriff Wherry called Katherine to have her send bus fare to send Gloria home.

Gloria was not happy to hear the news but for the next two days she lived with the Wherrys. In their small apartment Marion taught her to cook and the secret to crispy chicken. "Keep turning it, Gloria. Don't let the pieces sit too long in one place in the oil."

The last night in her temporary bedroom, Gloria slid again into sheets that smelled like the outdoors. She hated to go to sleep, knowing as each hour passed, she was closer to leaving.

After breakfast the next morning, everyone went to the jail and hugged. Even the sheriff's eyes watered. Sheriff Wherry gave Gloria one last ride in his squad car. She waved good-bye as she boarded the Greyhound bus, and with her nose pressed against the window, she cried the whole way home. She realized she had finally found normal and she had found it, of all places, in a South Dakota jail.

Mid-December 2008

"Hello?" said Sheriff Wherry, sounding older than Gloria remembered.

"Hi ... Sheriff Wherry?" Gloria told him her name. "You probably don't remember me, but I remember you and Marion. I'm calling just to say thanks for what you did for me when I was a teenager. You and

Marion took care of me when my boyfriend, Rick, was arrested for passing a bad check." Nervous, she forgot to allow him to speak and told him what a significant part Marion had played in her life. "I learned how to be a wife and mother because of Marion. She taught me how to set up a home, taught me how to cook and time meals so vegetables were done when the meat was. The two of you taught me what it takes to have a loving and good marriage. You two were such role models for us. I just wanted to say 'thank you' for being so kind to two terrified teenagers back in 1968." Silence filled the air and Gloria thought the cell phone signal had failed. "Hello? Sheriff Wherry?"

Sheriff Wherry's voice was wobbly. "You have no idea, Gloria, how many times Marion and I have thought about you over the years. I always wondered how you two made out in life."

"We've done pretty well, Sheriff. Rick and I will be married forty years next year."

"For goodness' sake. I can hardly believe it."

They talked for forty-five minutes, about Faulkton, about what transpired after she and Rick returned to St. Paul. She told him that they had two grown children. "Both Rick and I didn't have the best environments growing up, Sheriff. What we did learn, we learned from you and we put it all to good use."

"I'm happy to hear about your wonderful family," Sheriff said. "I'm touched that Marion and I had a positive influence on you two."

"I asked Rick a long time ago if he ever thought about Faulkton, Sheriff," Gloria said. "He told me that he thinks about it all the time. That you were the first adult who taught him something and you taught him through kindness. We've both wanted to thank you for a long time, but you know, Sheriff, when you get married and have children and you are running a business, you get engrossed in that. It wasn't until about ten years ago that we realized the degree to which you and Marion helped us." She told him about the Florida convention and the woman with the Faulkton badge. "I've put off calling until now, but today I just had to thank you."

He struggled with his emotions. "Many times Marion and I have said to each other, 'I wonder whatever happened to those two kids?' I tell you what. Marion and I have been a little sad, thinking it was going to be our worst Christmas ever because our kids aren't coming home this year."

His voice cracked and he paused. "This is the best Christmas present Marion and I have ever received. I still can't believe you're on the phone. I can't thank you enough for calling."

Neither wanted to stop exchanging memories, but Gloria had an appointment to keep in Duluth. They exchanged addresses, promised to send each other pictures, and hung up.

After Christmas, Gloria sent Sheriff Wherry newspaper clippings of their business and pictures of themselves and family. A letter from the sheriff came in Gloria's mail in late April 2009.

> *Dear Gloria,*
> *When you called, Marion was in the kitchen with me. She wondered what I had heard on the phone. She said she could have pushed me over with a feather from shock. She guessed it was you calling the more you and I talked …*

The envelope held published news accounts of his life and of him using his metal detection skills to locate objects from golfer Payne Stewart's plane when it went down near Faulkton. Beneath his signature Kenneth had written, "Marion died on April 4."

Gloria and Rick, in the summer of '68, had one foot in dysfunction but bumped into a different life in Faulkton, South Dakota. They were already damaged from their wounding world, but from their jail cells, they viewed a kind world, one they thought existed only on TV. The Wherrys guided them onto a road filled with hope and possibility.

When Gloria sat down next to a stranger on a Florida bus in 2007, her heart made a bridge to her past and tender memories. Pent-up words of gratitude overflowed when she thanked Sheriff Wherry for how he and Marion had specifically influenced her. She was so glad to have given her thanks while Marion was still alive.

Feeling gratitude and not expressing it
is like wrapping a gift and not giving it.

— Maya Angelou

We think we don't need to thank someone. We do. When Gloria gave her BlessBack, she unknowingly gave the Wherrys a wonderful Christmas present. We think the warm glow of good memories is enough but they only warm our hearts. "Silent gratitude," G. B. Stern said, "isn't much use to anyone."

We don't need a proper re-introduction to thank someone we knew a long time ago. Had Gloria waited longer to call, Marion would have missed the blessing.

We may think we need to make a big production to thank someone who helped us years ago, but Gloria simply made a call.

"The lesson in my BlessBack," Gloria wrote about her experience, "can be summed up with this: Never, never, never give up searching for that special someone in your past who deserves your blessing today."

If I can see further, it's because I've stood on the shoulders of giants.

— Sir Isaac Newton

Spontaneous BlessBacks

Heather Poole is a flight attendant based out of New York City. Near the end of a New York to Dallas flight, a little girl of nine years old handed Heather a card that said,

> *"Everyone on this plane that works on this plane is very kind and welcoming, comforting and makes me feel safe, happy and comfy, so thank you to everyone."*
> *Love, Fallyn*

BlessBacks are measured by the giver's heart, not by cost or size. Fallyn's note may seem a random act of kindness but she is actually living the BlessBack life, for Fallyn found the "extra" in an ordinary day.

Receiving thanks in the air travel industry is rare for Heather, so when it happens it's always appreciated. "In fact sometimes it's so appreciated, it feels weird, like, 'Do I really deserve this?'" Heather said. "Maybe that's because it's so rare to hear thanks that when you do, you feel like 'Wow, did I really do something special to deserve this?'"

Heather and her husband give BlessBacks, too. When she gave birth to their son, her husband ordered pizzas for all the nurses to thank them for their exceptional care and Heather sent flowers to the nurse who went above and beyond. "Giving thanks is so important," Heather said. "It affects people. When someone is nice to me, I want to be nice to others and so on, like a chain reaction."

Each day, the average person complains seventy times and has 45,000 negative thoughts. It's no wonder we're unhappy. The simplest way to counteract our negativity is to do the opposite.

Robert Holden is director of *The Happiness Project* in the United Kingdom. The typical "Stress Busters" he held weekly at his clinic consisted of attendees talking about their hard weeks. That all changed when Holden changed the rules and asked them to tell the group about something good, something in that past week that made them feel happy, or for which they felt grateful. Holden added another condition to their responses: no similar answers.

> *Each day, the average person complains seventy times and has 45,000 negative thoughts. It's no wonder we're unhappy.*

The group was reluctant at first but soon their attitudes shifted from complaining to those of being grateful. By the session's end, the group left with a renewed sense of well-being from viewing life from a gratefulness standpoint. Since that session, Holden has named this session the "Blessings" game. "Much of my therapeutic work with clients is, therefore, about helping people to rediscover the *trailing clouds of glory* [his italics]," Holden said in his book *Happiness Now! Timeless Wisdom for Feeling Good.*[1]

If we shift our thoughts to, "What is happening here that is good?" and then give a BlessBack, our brain will eventually create new passageways so that we will find the positive even when surrounded by stressful situations.

VALIDATION

One evening, Tom O'Brian watched his favorite TV show. During a commercial break, a news anchor gave a public service announcement encouraging viewers to thank a teacher who had made a difference in their lives.

Tom thought of *Futuristics,* a special course he took in high school twenty-five years ago. Leonard Bielke, his teacher, had designed and implemented the new course. The program was experimental and structured around the concept of future-thinking. It combined English, history, geography and math courses. Tom was a junior when Mr. Bielke asked him to participate in the course. Tom flourished under Mr. Bielke's instruction and loved the class. He wrote his final paper on the future demographics of the city of Richfield. Pleased with Tom's work, Mr. Bielke sent it to the city planner. The planner invited Tom to his office and asked him how he made his projections. Tom told him it was Mr. Bielke who taught him to look at trends and extrapolate data to predict the city's growth.

Two months after hearing the PSA on TV, Tom stopped at a fast-food restaurant for breakfast. Already late for work, he knew he had to hurry.

Standing in line, he spotted a man who looked like Henry Kissinger. Tom thought again of the PSA and Mr. Bielke. On second look, Tom realized the man was Mr. Bielke.

Okay, he thought. *I'm going to stretch myself.* He stepped out of line and tapped Mr. Bielke's shoulder. Mr. Bielke turned to face him.

"Hi, Mr. Bielke. I'm Tom O'Brian ... I was one of your students in the '70s," he said. He shared how the organizational and forward-thinking skills he learned from him forged his career path. "I just wanted to thank you for everything I learned from you."

"Why, Tom O'Brian. Yes, I remember you," Mr. Bielke said. "You wouldn't believe how many years of effort I put into that program to make it work. Thank you for thanking me. I want you to know you've made my day." He shook Tom's hand, turned and ordered his food and sat down in a booth.

A few minutes later, he walked to Tom in line. "Would you like to join me for breakfast?"

"I would love to but I'm already late for work," Tom said. "Thank you for asking me, though."

"You know," Mr. Bielke said. "I'd like to change what I said. You just didn't make my day. You made my life."

Tom stood there, choked up. "I was astounded by the impact of my words," he later said. "I felt honored back by him. I was so glad I stepped out and took a risk."

For twenty-five years, Mr. Bielke had wondered if the ideas presented in his future-thinking course had made an impact on students' lives. Because one person, on a chance encounter, expressed his thanks, Mr. Bielke was validated. All it took was receiving recognition and thanks for advancing another's career.

Valid means *possessed of health and strength.* When we validate others with a BlessBack, we show we recognize their value. We make visible the good we see. We renew their life's purpose and substantiate their existence by telling them the good ways in which they have affected us. And we, in the afterglow of giving, are validated, too.

BEING NOTICED

Dave Schneider was 5 foot 10 and 150 pounds of brawn as a teenager in the late 1950s. His parents divorced when he was seven and not long afterward, his life on the north side of Minneapolis included financially supporting a sickly and morose mother and rescuing his alcoholic father from bars and drunken stupors. He ached to flee from "I wish you'd never been born" rants from his mother. He wanted to forget that he had a father who never showed up when he promised to spend a Saturday together.

Things were not much better at school. Dave wasn't a good student; he hated school and wanted to join the military at fifteen. Mr. Casperson was vice-principal of Central High School. When he learned Dave planned to fake his age to sign up for the military, he called Dave into his office. "I hear you're going to register for the army," he said.

Dave's face didn't flinch. He intentionally crossed his arms to bulge his toned muscles, ever-ready to take on the enemy, even if the enemy was the principal and the combat zone was school. "Yeah, that's right."

"I'll make a deal with you," Mr. Casperson said. "If you'll agree to wait to sign up until you've got your diploma, I'll do what I can to help you enlist."

Trust an adult? And yet, Dave had heard Mr. Casperson had offered to help other male students. And unlike his father, Mr. Casperson had kept his promises and helped them graduate. But another two years of trying to wrap his brain around school seemed too high of a mountain to climb.

"What do you say, Dave. Willing to give it a try?"

He heard himself say a quiet, "Yeah."

Telling the story now, fifty-five years later, Dave says, "Mr. Casperson was the first person who saw something in me, something that I could give to the world. He was the first person who believed in me."

Both parties kept their word. With the aid of Mr. Casperson, Dave received the direction and help he needed to graduate. He wasn't alone in his struggle to get out of a bad side of town and difficult home life. Five other young men at his high school received a hand up and out of that life. Of those, two men, Dave and Jim, managed to break the cycle of crime and poverty. Dave did join the army and became a non-commissioned officer at the age of eighteen. Upon his discharge after three years, he worked full-time and went to night school for six years, gaining expertise in the electrical and electronic fields. He ended his career running the computer department at a prominent utility company.

Dave's fellow classmate, Jim, followed in Mr. Casperson's footsteps and became principal of a 2,000-student high school.

Both Dave and Jim met again at Mr. Casperson's funeral in 1993. Dave told one of Casperson's sons, "You have no idea the impact your father made on our lives," Dave said. "He was the first person to ever really care about me."

If you are waiting for the courage to BlessBack someone, pretend this is what your recipient is calling out to you right now:

> *Dear You,*
>
> *Put away your fears. I would love to hear from you and what you have to say. I will be touched beyond measure by your sincere heart and your willingness to find me to tell me what I have meant to you. Sometimes I wonder if I, the un-celebrity, the un-rich, have made any difference in the world at all. You can change that in an instant for me. In fact, you may be the person who gives me the courage to BlessBack someone in my life if you show me how it's done.*

THE RESET BUTTON

Marty Schutrop was at a dinner meeting when a man started a conversation. Introductions began and when the man heard Marty's last name he said, "Schutrop. Would that be the Schutrops from Hopkins?"

Marty nodded.

"You don't happen to know a David Schutrop, do you?"

"Yes I do. He's my brother."

The man, overcome with emotion, sat down at their table. His eyes filled with tears and his voice shook as he spoke. "When I was a teenager in the early '60s, a bully picked on me because I had polio and limped. One day, this guy knocked my crutch away and I crashed to the ground. Your brother happened to be standing near me and took care of that guy so that I was never bothered again. Your brother single-handedly changed the course of my life from that moment on. Please thank him for me."

When someone takes the time to tell us about something good we have done, it is like someone has pressed the reset button inside of us.

We live so close to ourselves that we cannot see the good acts or kindnesses we do. When we don't see or hear, we tend to subconsciously discount or disqualify our lives as being boring, trite, insignificant. We believe the lie we tell ourselves, that nothing of exception happens in our lives. When someone takes the time to tell us about something good we have done, it is like someone has pressed the reset button inside of us. We are refreshed, ready to carry on again.

To the world you might be one person.
To one person, you just might be the world.

— Unknown

INSTILLING DREAMS

1988 might conjure up images of banana clips, neon legwarmers and acid-washed jeans. It was all of those for Jill Hildebrandt, but it was also the first time she voted, the year she began college, and the year she met Elaine.

Elaine Larson was a graduate teaching assistant for *Acting for Everyone*, one of the first college courses Jill took at her Minnesota university.

Elaine had wiry, silver hair, wide-eyed expressions and animated gesticulation when she talked. After Jill's first monologue performance in that course, Elaine enthusiastically came up to her, grabbed her hands, looked into her eyes and said, "Jill, you have a gift. You have a gift for acting and need to do something about it." She asked Jill to become a theatre major and audition for shows.

But school, plus a thirty-five-hour work week, curbed that dream. "While I couldn't follow through at that time with what Elaine had said to me," Jill said, "Elaine gave me a gift on two levels. No one had ever told me I had a gift for anything. Elaine took the time to tell me I was talented as an actress and inspired me later in life."

Eight years later, buoyed by Elaine's words, Jill pursued her graduate degree in Performance Studies and later took acting classes in New York City. She has since moved back to Minneapolis. As a full-time professor, wife and mother, Jill performs when she can but Elaine's words have stayed with her. "Elaine inspired me as a teacher as I work to find the gifts in my students," Jill said.

One student from the South side of Chicago stands out for Jill. She was in Jill's *Performing Cultures* course at a large Illinois university and on the weekends went home to take care of her ailing grandfather with her grandmother. After her first performance, Jill wrote on her evaluation sheet, "Nicole, you have a gift for acting, and even if you don't pursue a theatre major (she was a Mortuary Science major at the time), I hope you try to continue performing."

Two weeks later, Nicole came running to Jill in class and said, "I was so excited by what you wrote that I auditioned for the theatre department student showcases. I didn't get cast, but I made it to callbacks. I did that because you motivated me. No one has ever said I had a gift. I ran home and told everyone that my teacher thinks I have a gift." A few years later, the student emailed Jill, thanking her again for that experience. "She said my words changed her life and gave her confidence," Jill said. "Exactly what Elaine gave to me when she said those similar words some ten years earlier."

...we can create a directional pause in others and help them to see the potential they cannot see for themselves.

"Be an opener of doors" is the motto at a local university. Elaine helped Jill open the door to her future life by recognizing her talent. Elaine's words helped Jill to pursue her acting gifts and make her dreams of acting on stage in New York City become real. Elaine's words also inspired Jill to give BlessBacks of her own.

It's hard to fathom that we can affect another's direction in life but as Gloria's, Dave's and Jill's stories have shown, we can create a directional pause in others and help them to see the potential they cannot see for themselves.

LATVIAN GOLD

During World War II, the Russians advanced into Latvia and displaced an entire country. Inta Klans was only two when her father, Adolff, bribed a German captain of an ocean-going vessel with bacon and cigarettes as he pulled anchor in Liepāja, Latvia. "The ship was leaving and they threw a cargo net out. My mom, dad, brother and I jumped into it and that is how we got out of there," Inta said. The family fled to Poland in 1944, finding refuge on land owned by Inta's grandfather in Dunsig (now Gdansk). Within weeks, the Russians invaded that country as well and they had to flee again.

This time the family fled by horse and wagon with the Germans. "The German army was retreating and we followed them," Inta said. The German government was willing to take in refugees. They assigned the Klanses to a family that owned a little bar in Amelinghausen, Germany. "They were ordered to give us a room to stay in," Inta said, "and we stayed there for nine months. They were very kind to us. Mother helped milk cows. Our family became very close to these people. We stayed in their guest house. Today, the bar has become a beautiful five-star restaurant."

When the war ended, Germany split into four zones, American, French, Russian and British. Amelinghausen, in northern Germany, was in the British zone. "Displaced Person camps were created," Inta said, "because we didn't have a country anymore." The Klans family lived as Displaced Persons for more than six years, moving from camp to camp. Each one had Latvian doctors, lawyers and teachers and Inta was able to go to Latvian school.

The family shared barracks with another family and eight soldiers. Inta Klans still remembers the pea soup served at the refugee camp. "We called it 'green horror' in Latvian because it tasted awful," she said.

Though the Klanses lived in the British zone, they could not go to England because England did not accept refugee families, especially maimed ones, and Adolff had a crippled hand. "My father wanted to come to America," Inta said, "but US immigration laws at that time were such that it didn't want handicapped people. You needed to be able to work and be able to take care of yourself, and somebody had to promise you a job before you could leave the camp."

Others were turned down if they had tuberculosis, cancer or a venereal disease. "We were constantly checked to make sure we weren't diseased," Inta, who was eight at the time, said. "They'd line us up and spray DDT down our collars to make sure we didn't have lice and wouldn't spread it."

Latvia is ninety percent Lutheran so when word came to the Klans family that the First Lutheran Church of Williston, North Dakota would sponsor seven Latvian families, they were thrilled. They arrived in August 1951, owning nothing but the clothes on their backs.

Though Inta's parents did not know English, the father of the sponsoring family spoke German, as did Inta's father, and the two families found a way to communicate. Members of the church donated canned goods and a Bible camp donated beds. Her mother labored as a silk presser at a dry cleaner while her father worked at Williston Transfer and Storage Company.

Inta and her brother Aivars went to a public school for the first time.

Inta now was nine but placed in the second grade because she did not know English. Her teacher, Miss Manger, made it her personal challenge to teach the children English. "She was just an exceptional person and went out of her way," Inta said. Days into the school year, students poked fun at Inta for her clothes and laced, high-top boots. "We looked different," Inta said, "and I couldn't understand English. I didn't want to take my coat off because people would see my shoes. I would not come out of the coat room because the kids were laughing at me."

Miss Manger brought her into the room and talked to the children. "Even though I couldn't understand what she said, you could tell they were being told not to make fun of me," Inta said. From that day on, the children treated the Klans children kindly. Inta still sees her classmates, now lifelong friends.

When Inta and Aivars moved to junior high, Miss Manger sent them cards and small gifts. "She never, ever forgot us. She wanted us to have a good life. She wanted us to succeed."

Miss Manger was also their Sunday School teacher. "You could tell Miss Manger's whole goal in life was to mold young people and to teach them what was right," Inta said.

Inta moved to Minneapolis in 1957 because of its strong Latvian community. She married and had two children. In 1984, Inta and Aivars started talking about their memories of Williston and Miss Manger and before long, they decided to go for a visit. They found Miss Manger living at a nursing home in North Dakota. "We are Inta and Aivars Klans. Do you remember us?" they asked her.

"Of course," Miss Manger said.

"We just wanted to stop and say 'hi,'" Inta said.

"We just wanted to thank you for all you did for us," Aivars said.

"I didn't do enough," Miss Manger said.

Aivars and Inta started to tear up because they knew just how much she had done for them. "When you have somebody like that in your life," Inta said, "you want to please them. You want to be good."

Miss Manger has passed away but Inta is so grateful she took the time to drive eleven hours to see her second-grade teacher. "There is a phrase in Latvian that describes Miss Manger. Jūs esiet zelta cilvēks. 'You are a golden person.' It is a phrase reserved only for those who do something special. It is the ultimate compliment a Latvian can give a person. Miss Manger will always be a golden person. She will always be in my heart."

THE GRATITUDE VISIT

Martin Seligman, a main figure in the positive psychology field and a founding father of a master's program in the field at the University of Pennsylvania, is convinced gratitude is an essential component to a satisfied life. Based on a student's suggestion, he began his teaching semester in 2001 by holding gratitude visits. The process was simple. Students asked those who had made a positive impact on their lives — relatives and friends — to come to class one evening. One by one, the students read their thank-filled letters to their guests, letting them know how they had influenced them.[2]

In an interview with *The Philadelphia Inquirer* Seligman said about the gathering. "There was lots of weeping and hugging. It was the best night of teaching I've experienced in forty years." Seligman believes reading students' letters aloud contributed to the giver and receiver feeling content and satisfied.[3]

"Part of the magic of the gratitude visit," Seligman said, "is that it's contagious. It's a good deed that breeds others, so that gratefulness spreads. Positive gratitude creates a positive life."[4]

Today, Seligman continues the exercise, but he also teaches the process to life coaches, psychologists, and those in academia. One of those in attendance in the spring of 2003, Michael Auerbach, said afterward, "It's not only a benefit for someone else, it really lifts your own spirits. It forces you to slow down and realize what you have to be thankful for."[5]

May the Lord bless you and keep you,
May the Lord make His face to shine upon you and be gracious to you
May the Lord lift up His countenance upon you
and give you peace.

— Numbers 6:24

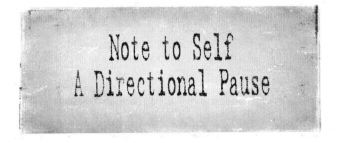

Note to Self
A Directional Pause

THE IDEAL – A DIRECTIONAL PAUSE

Benediction has its roots in *benedicere, bene,* meaning well, *dicere,* to speak or speak well of. In the Christian religion, it means to invoke a blessing from God upon another.

In the same way someone speaks a blessing over us, we too, can act and live our lives as a benediction to others. Sheriff Wherry and Marion spoke a benediction of goodness into Gloria and Rick's lives simply by their actions. They were kind, telling the teenagers of the goodness they saw in them; they gave them shelter and food, and invited them into their lives. Most of all, the sheriff and Marion showed the young couple the value in taking a directional pause. It's the same affect the teachers in this chapter evoked when they inspired their students to contemplate their course and reach for their dreams.

THE LOOK BACK

Sometimes we need a harbor, sometimes we need a foghorn, sometimes we need a salty old dog to show us how we've strayed, give us a course correction, or to help us find normal.

If you look for parallels between Gloria and Rick's story and your own, where do you find commonality?

Was there a time you discovered you'd set course in the wrong direction?

Was it circumstances, your choices, or some of each that caused you to stray?

Who presented a directional pause and how did he or she help you correct your course or speak, through actions, a benediction over you?

THE INVITATION

"Golden" is used a lot in our country. Photographers use "the golden hour" to describe the first and last hours when the horizons are at their lustrous best. We use it to describe opportunities, a triangle, a ratio, silence, a state, dogs, beer, anniversaries, and birthdays, to name a few.

Most of us are familiar with the Bible's golden rule: "Do to others what you would want them to do to you." The golden rule isn't about a governing sense of rule; rather, it's a way of life. It's an ethical code that asks you to not make yourself an exception to the rule but to treat others in the same way you desire. The result is we build up one another.

A BLESSBACK COURSE OF ACTION
Who are the top three people in your life you would call "a golden person"?

If they used the golden rule as a standard, how so?

How have you taken the ways they lived the golden rule and applied it to your life?

Go to your calendar and designate a day in each of the next three months and write on the date, "Thank my Golden Person today."

BENEDICTION

Help me to be present in each moment.
For I want to be conscious of each day's golden hours,
to treat others as I want to be treated.
May I be a candle to someone who has lost the way,
a hand to guide, a shoulder for another to stand on,
mindful always of the golden people in my life.

Normal day,
Let me be aware
of the treasure
you are.

— Mary Jean Iron
Notes From a Traveler Afar

CHAPTER SIX
BlessBacks Build Community

*There is no power for change greater
than a community discovering what it cares about.*

— Margaret J. Wheatley

The soybeans and corn seed arrived ready to plant in April 2009 at the Waxdahl farm in Flandreau, South Dakota, but the weather and family circumstances would prevent their sowing.

Planting nearly two square miles of seed was almost too much for the Waxdahl sons. The rainy spring and drenched fields only delayed the process. It would take weeks of hard and steady work, from early morning to night, to get the crops planted.

Florence, Gordon, Don and their families inherited their parents' farm. Florence rented her portion to her brothers, who were both in their sixties. Gordon had been sick for five days with flu-like symptoms and wasn't getting better.

Don, too, had other concerns. He and his wife Rosanne were headed toward Rochester, Minnesota for test results on his prostate, and thoughts of his wife's own upcoming colon surgery had him worried. How could he tend to her and help his brother plant two sections of crops? More than a half-million dollars in crop value was at stake.

Don and Rosanne came out of his doctor's appointment at Mayo Clinic that spring day having to make another adjustment. He had cancer and, along with Rosanne, faced surgery in June. The couple was just beginning to process the news as they left the hospital when Don's cellphone buzzed. He checked his voice mail and listened to a surreal message from Gordon's family. "You have to get to Sioux Falls right away or you will not see your brother alive."

"How can a man who is never sick now be on his death bed?" Don asked his wife as the two rushed home.

When Don and Rosanne reached the Sioux Falls hospital, they found Gordon unresponsive, kept alive by a machine that pressed air into his lungs.

On April 23, Gordon left this world, leaving behind a grief-stricken family. He was sixty-four.

After learning of Gordon's passing, neighbors came by. "I can hardly say it," Florence said recently, her voice constricting as she recounted the family's story. "They told us, 'Your crops will be planted and taken care of so you don't need to worry about it.'" The next day, neighboring farmers learned of Don and Rosanne's impending surgeries and came again. "You don't need to worry about the crops; they will be harvested too."

The farmers refused to allow Florence and her brothers' wives to feed them and refused reimbursement for the hundreds of dollars in diesel fuel used. Within days, surrounding farmers had planted the Waxdahl family's crops.

"Farmers have always done this for each other but this was so much," Florence said. "And all these people had their own land to plant and were also late getting their crops in because it was such a wet spring."

Once Don and Rosanne had their successful surgeries, the Waxdahl family made a plan. "We couldn't repay them for their efforts," Florence said. "But we could thank them."

They invited the fifty people involved in planting their crops to a June dinner at Mad Mary's restaurant in Flandreau. "We had door prizes and everyone got a magnet that said, 'You are all hearts! With sincere thanks from the Waxdahl family.'" Florence and her family went from table to table, thanking their friends. The farmers brushed off the Waxdahls' gratefulness. "Oh, it was nothing, I was glad to do it," was the typical response. "Oh, I didn't do much," or "It was only right." One farmer said, "We're glad to do it. That's what we're here for. You'd do it for us."

For Florence, receiving help from farming families was a humbling experience. "When it was first happening I couldn't do anything but cry. It's so humbling, but it's so wonderful," she said. "You have to accept the help because we had to have it. All we could say was 'thank you.'"

No one who achieves success does so without acknowledging the help of others.
The wise and confident acknowledge this help with gratitude.

— Alfred North Whitehead

Lynn G. Underwood, professor of biomedical humanities at Hiram College, uses the phrase "compassionate love" to explain altruism. Underwood believes compassionate love includes making space for others to give. Yale physician Alan Mermann also believes in the "importance of creating spaces for others to give," and that "being open to receiving does not diminish our gift of self."[1]

...compassionate love includes making space for others to give.

Though not intentional, the death of a loved one, the size of their land and the weather were all factors that opened up space for the Flandreau community to offer compassionate love. Had the circumstances been different, they may have missed experiencing what being given a BlessBack felt like: love expressed compassionately.

Because love, hospitality and generosity were already in place in the people of Flandreau, a caring and concerned community had naturally formed. When the Waxdahls were in crisis, the community's connectedness resulted in altruistic action.

THE *HAPPY* FILM

Director Roko Belic and author Eiji Shimizu traveled to fourteen countries over a four-year span to study what makes people happy. Their documentary, *Happy*, looked at people in all walks of life to find common denominators of happiness. Among those they interviewed included a Cajun fisherman, bushmen in the Kalahari Desert, a drug addict, and a person in the last stages of life.

The happiest were not the richest, famous or most physically beautiful people. Shimizu said in an interview with CNN Asia that "happiness comes from a sense of 'connectedness' with something bigger than oneself, such as family, community, religion, nature, ancestry or the universe in general."

The filmmakers were so affected by their findings, they made changes in their own lives. One began to surf again, reconnecting with nature;

another moved from his 17,000-square-foot home to a mobile home and now bikes to work. He has become involved in his community in a way he never bothered to before. Still another quit his high-salary job to be involved in a community with other creative people.

So, it's what we value — compassion, cooperation and wanting to make the world a better place — Belic added, that leads to happiness, not the things money can buy.[2]

Janet Gibson, a licensed marriage and family therapist, said that intimacy breeds conflict. It's true. We go about life in scrunched elevators, coach seats, and drive on streets overflowing with traffic. We annoy each other to no end. But we need each other and we need each other's compassionate love speaking blessings upon us.

Sometimes it seems we are each creating our little fiefdoms. It's easy to do. What's hard to do is to commit ourselves to serve our neighborhoods and communities. But we must. "While we are, this is," wrote C. S. Lewis in *The Problem of Pain*. "If we lose this, we lose all."[3]

The early church "gave to anyone as he had need." When we give physical expressions of BlessBacks as a community, we act as God would have us. And we all have needs, whether it's something big like neighbors who plant your crops or another who collects your mail when you're out of town.

Life is meant to be truly lived within the harvest of people.

Being in community with each other brings purpose to us all. It is in our nature to desire community with one another. We thrive with humanity's agrarian hugs and concrete kisses of kindness. Life is meant to be truly lived within the harvest of people.

In my belief, a harvest is a legacy,
for very often what you reap is, in the way of small miracles,
more than you consciously know you have sown.

— Faith Baldwin

Do the Local Motion With Me

Just before leaving the house with my husband Rick to meet another couple for a quick mid-week meal, I turned on the five o'clock news to learn that the I-35W Bridge, twenty miles from our house, had collapsed. The bridge was an entryway into the city carrying 140,000 cars across its nearly 500-foot-span across the Mississippi River. On that terrible night, August 1, 2007, chaos clogged the highway in both directions; it was rush hour, compounded by twenty-five-thousand people heading to a Twins game, when the bridge gave way. Cameras showed the emotions the reporters themselves could not hide and we who watched all felt right along with them their disbelief, fright, shock, and worry. Reporters interviewed frightened joggers, who narrowly escaped death as they ran underneath the bridge. Live video from a news helicopter showed a yellow school bus hanging at a precarious forty-degree angle on a concrete section of the fallen bridge sixty feet above the water. A young man named Jeremy helped evacuate the scared students from the bus. It was hard to watch the rescue. One couldn't help but picture the concrete chunk collapsing into the water before all the kids were safe.

Below them, the US Coast Guard worked frantically to reach victims trapped in submerged cars near treacherous wing dams hidden in the water underneath the bridge.

Rick and I reluctantly went to the pizzeria to meet our friends. Two flat-screened televisions, each on a different channel, showed images of distraught, scared people. The tragedy preempted local and national news.

The four of us hardly talked. When we did, it was to find out if loved ones were okay. A cousin called from Indiana. My husband's cousin called from Seattle, happy to get ahold of us. I called my mother and one brother but could still not reach my other brother, Mark, who was with his wife and four children coming home from northern Minnesota. I knew his route meant crossing that bridge.

For two hours our cell phones spat "All circuits are busy" as we tried to reach friends who worked in downtown Minneapolis, the epicenter of the catastrophe.

Later that night, I finally reached Mark. They had stopped a half-hour from the bridge for a quick "pit stop," then continued on their way. Two miles from the bridge, they came to a dead halt and wondered what was going on when someone came running down the freeway yelling, "The 35-W bridge is down!"

Thirteen people died that day.

When tragedies of this magnitude occur, whether in a city or a suburb, whether we are old or young, a civilian or government worker, our compassion pours out. We could not help but cry when days later we heard a recording of a woman's last phone call home before she drowned, swallowed up by the Mississippi. My friend lost her co-worker. Another friend learned a wife and four children who lived down her block had lost a husband and dad. We were all devastated.

In the days that followed, every network and cable news show descended on Minneapolis and broadcasted from buildings overlooking the broken bridge. They interviewed Governor Pawlenty and our US senators, Amy Klobuchar and Norm Coleman. Even President Bush came to the state.

Pastors united and planned a huge worship service for the upcoming weekend, but Rick and I had plans with friends to go up to our cabin. We arrived home late on the night of August 5 and I was anxious to see how our community was faring, but the only live program on at 10:30 p.m. was *Rosen's Sports Sunday* on our local channel. I turned it on, expecting a Vikings training camp overview, but what I viewed was a show straight from Mr. Rosen's heart about Jeremy and his rescue of those kids on the bus.

I penned him a note the next day.

> *Dear Mr. Rosen:*
>
> *I just wanted to say thank you for your program last night. I saw a reporter's "heart." I saw your compassion for all those who were affected by the collapse of the bridge, yet to me, a non-sports person, you built a bridge to me in I saw that reporters, as strong as they try to be on-camera, are just as real and full of emotion as the rest of us regarding this tragedy, and you care about this community called the Twin Cities as much as we do.*
>
> *Please thank the other reporters on your program who covered the tragedy and your entire news organization for showing what true sportsmanship looks like. You are all heroes in my eyes for your own bravery and sacrifice to get the story told. I appreciate all that you do. I shed a few tears as you handed Jeremy a certificate to get his car fixed, arranged for him to begin studying again at Dunwoody, assisted in getting caps, etc. from sports clubs around town for the kids on that bus, and that you dedicated a full half-hour to a young man who captained his team of young people to safety.*

Several weeks ago the Minneapolis Star Tribune had an article about altruism that when people see it being carried out in others, viewers' brains are affected. It is as if the viewers themselves had done the altruistic deed. I was skeptical, yet that is exactly what happened for me while watching your show. I was moved and just wanted you to know that.

An e-letter came the same day, shortly before WCCO's 5 p.m. news broadcast.

August 6, 2007

Julie,
I don't know where to start. I can't thank you enough for your incredibly thoughtful email. When I read about Jeremy's situation in Friday's St. Paul paper, unable to afford to continue his education at Dunwoody Institute, I said to myself, 'This can't happen, we can't afford to have terrific young men like this fall through our cracks.' The Dunwoody folks responded immediately and after numerous phone conversations with Jeremy's relatives, I was honored that he said yes to coming in last night, especially after he said no to the president for his photo op on Saturday afternoon.

I didn't meet Jeremy until he came to our studio last night, and once the cameras go away, I plan on seeing him a lot more. He has an opportunity, by continuing his education and becoming an auto mechanic, to be an amazing role model for so many others. He already is. I learned a lot from this twenty-year-old in a half hour last night. I told him that a lot of good will come out of this bad situation and he'll have many years to share his wisdom with others.
Thank you again. Mark Rosen

I include my letter to show how easy writing a letter or email of thanks is to do, just *because*. We can be people of "because." We can act or write others when we see them doing something good. "Be causal," by blessing and thanking others with a BlessBack in your neighborhoods, communities and places where you work. It won't be long before a bond of compassion forms.

Kristen Ballum lost Sherry Engebretsen, her friend and co-worker, in the I-35W bridge collapse. "What I remember most is hearing the news about Sherry when only a handful of people knew ... then I stared out the window at work and collapsed to the floor."

Kristen works on the executive floor so she saw immediately how the company responded. "Company leaders gave co-workers room to maneuver through their loss and pain. They showed us it was okay to mourn through our grief," she said.

The memorial service, with Sherry's family present, was held in the company's auditorium. "Observing how our company united and responded to her death moved me to my knees in gratitude," she said. "It was awash in hope, humor and truth. I was never so proud of the company I work for as I was then because the caring was so authentic and filled with respect and bathed in compassion for the family and for us."

Let kindness become your cause and it will affect those around you.

BlessBacks: The Power to Persuade

In this day and age where school district budget cuts seem to be a battle every year, writing a letter just may affect what programs stay.

May 23, 1994

Dear Dr. Swenson,
I would like to extend my thanks to you for the wonderful education I have received at Stillwater Area High School. It has been a very enriching experience.

Most of all, I would like to thank you for the instruction I got from Mrs. Jacobs. When I began my years at the Marsh Street campus, I didn't exactly know if I fit in. I wouldn't say that I was shy, but I was very lonely and depressed. The stage had always been an interest of mine, but I wasn't sure if I could act in a professional high school production. Nevertheless, I tried out for the 1992 fall play, To Kill a Mockingbird. *I didn't know if I would get a part. If I did, I was sure I would be shuffled in the background. Imagine my surprise when I was given the part of Dill, a major role in the play. The fact that someone would have that confidence in me was overwhelming. I put a lot of energy into the role of Dill. I was constantly being complimented, while also receiving constructive criticism so that I could do the best I possibly could to totally fulfill the part. Along the way, I also made a lot of friends that I have kept throughout high school. I have taken part in an improvisational theatre company and have taken courses at the Phipps Center for the Arts, but I have never received a better education in theatre than from Mrs. Jacobs.*

It does not end with me, either. Mrs. Jacobs has been a great inspiration for a number of students. There have been a number of people whom I have seen who were shy, unsure of themselves, confused and depressed, and avoiding any contact with people. Through theatre, they have learned how to express themselves, and gained a number of friends in the process.

I have been in many plays since To Kill a Mockingbird. *I have played a fidgety old man in* Scapino!, *the kind Monsignor Myriel in* Les Misérables, *a concerned father in* Rest Stop, *and a potential murder victim in the comedy* Arsenic and Old Lace. *I have also served in publicity and video production for many of the plays, and have also taken Mrs. Jacobs' Introduction to Theatre class. But my favorite memory is still the role of Dill. Dill was a person who didn't know if he belonged and was very unsure of himself. In the friends he makes, he finds a place where he is accepted, appreciated, and loved. That is exactly what happened to me when I became involved in Mrs. Jacobs' drama program. Not only did I make friendships that will last a long time, but I also obtained invaluable instruction from Mrs. Jacobs, who is not only a fantastic teacher and theatre director, but also a great role model.*

I am graduating now. I plan to attend Hamline University in the fall. My experiences at Stillwater Area High School have given me the courage to be involved with Hamline's theatre program. I will take everything I have learned from Mrs. Jacobs and use it throughout my college years. The drama program is an essential part to our high school, and so is Mrs. Jacobs.
Sincerely, Scott Davis

Scott's letter was one of hundreds the school district received from a community upset with budget cuts. His, though, was the catalyst for the school superintendent to keep Mrs. Jacobs' job and the theater budget in place the following year. Children play an important role in education, and when they write BlessBack letters to people who make decisions, their voices can make a difference in our communities.

Time Warp, a science show on the Discovery Channel, featured colleagues at Massachusetts' Institute of Technology who explained what happens when a raindrop lands on water. Viewed at normal speed with the naked eye, the drop looked like it immediately merged into the puddle. But when they slowed the camera to 2000 frames per second, we saw what really happened.[4]

The drop briefly sat on top of the water, then bounced repeatedly before it permanently integrated into the water.

In a slow motion, close-up shot, the camera showed the dropper release a drop. The drop landed on the water's surface, causing the surface to compress like a meteor compresses the earth upon impact. Though invisible to the eye, as the drop descended, it pushed aside a thin layer of air between the drop and the water.

Much of the drop was absorbed into the water, but a smaller remnant of the drop was pinched off, creating a droplet. This droplet, like the drop before it, bounced into the air before it hit the water, again, creating a smaller crater-like impact. The droplets repeated the process until they coalesced into the water. Viewed in slow motion, the drop and its droplets looked like little balls bouncing on an elastic plastic sheet.

John Bush, professor of applied mathematics at MIT, explained on the cable program why the drop and droplets bounced back up into the air: "When drops coalesce, waves generate at the point of contact and they sweep upward and apply a force which lifts the drops off the surface."

In other words, what Bush is saying is that water has surface tension. The impact of the drop makes circular waves upon that tension. The waves cause the drop to react much like people on descent toward a trampoline; their force sends the drop back up into the air. "It's the effect that allows insects to walk on water and water drops to hold together," said the *Time Warp* narrator. "This cycle happens again and again until the droplet is small enough to be completely absorbed."

DROPS OF GRATITUDE: A CAUSE AND EFFECT

The world of "me" that is visible to the naked eye shows a middle-aged woman who seems to function just fine. Upon meeting me, you would surmise that my act is together.

But I have a "me" that, unless you're one of my closest and dearest of friends, isn't seen. Sometimes, in fact, I don't even see that me, nor do I understand her. Earlier in the book, I let you see a part of her – the one who was afraid to play in the game of life. The one who was only able to believe again her father's motto "Who's more fun than people?" when she acted to thank those people for their influence.

I had to release myself from that dropper, so to speak, before I could affect the surface of my world. Staying inside did no one, not even me, any good. Only when I moved from being inert to animated, could and did change happen. Only when I had a worthwhile cause — giving people thanks — could I affect others. Only when I released myself from my self-created womb did I become alive and make an impression of change.

If we use the raindrops example, the order of action goes like this: The water drop not only dispersed the water beneath it; it moved the air around it before it landed. The visible (the drop) moved the invisible (air) and the invisible (air) moved the visible (the puddle).

Just as the drop caused the air to move, we may never see the chain reaction caused by our giving another person our gratitude. But, like air, just because we can't see it doesn't mean a chain reaction is not there. We know air exists because we see its effects when the wind riffles through leaves, trees bend and whip in a hurricane, and waves claw to shore.

The same is true for gratitude. We may not see the effects of one single gift of gratitude, but if we listen for it, we will hear the effects of it in the news, our communities, schools and the world.

> We may not see the effects of one single gift of gratitude, but if we listen for it, we will hear the effects of it in the news, our communities, schools and the world.

Psychologist Ross Buck says that when gratitude is modeled, especially early in a child's life, it tends to stay with a person for life. "This kind of gratitude involves a personal relationship associated with love and bonding," Buck writes. "Th[e] giving benefits and receiving benefits are mutually supportive. Literally, the more you give, the more you get."[5]

"Altruism" takes its meaning from the Latin root *alter,* other, as it relates to "the other" being in need. Stephen Post and the editors of *Altruism and Altruistic Love* state that "An altruist intends and acts for the other's sake rather than as a means to public recognition or internal well-being."[6] This explains why Jeremy, once off the collapsed bridge, declined a meeting with heads of state.

Our brains are wired so that when we see an altruistic act, we experience its warm glow. When Ty Pennington and the *Extreme Home Makeover* crowd shouted "Move that bus!" and we saw the joy-filled expressions on the homeowners' faces when they saw what a group of construction workers, designers and the community built for them, we experienced the good feelings as though we were there, too.

Recent findings suggest the more you live altruistically and make the practice a habit, the more easily you will experience altruistic feelings when you perceive others practicing gratitude.

The more you experience giving, the more loved and bonded to others you will feel. A BlessBack is the Great Give-Get. The act of a BlessBack feels great and it spreads goodness into the world. At the same time, when you authentically thank, you will receive the afterglow of your altruistic act.

When we release our droplets of thanks, we cause a ripple effect and before you know it, others will join the BlessBack dance.

Here is an example of a rain drop metaphor as it relates to altruism and giving BlessBacks.

Across the globe, people watched news shows on January 12, 2010 when Haiti's horrific 7.0 magnitude earthquake killed more than 200,000 people. American cell phone providers came together, and for two days, they allowed donors to send a free text submitting donations to their favorite charity. Within that period, charities received more than $5 million in donations, surpassing the 2004 text donations for Hurricane Katrina and Tsunami relief.

When a headline tells us that cell phone companies sacrificed revenue to unite in altruism, we want to give, too. I felt good hearing how many people gave ten dollars towards helping Haitians; When I gave my own donation, I felt very much aware of the selfless community I had joined

— those who needed and those who responded to that need.

When we release our droplets of thanks, we cause a ripple effect and before you know it, others will join the BlessBack dance. Like us, they too, will change their world and the surface of their world. Every droplet of kindness and goodness matters and as it does, our community is built of compassionate love.

Gratitude is something of which none of us can give too much.
For on the smiles, the thanks we give,
our little gestures of appreciation,
our neighbors build their philosophy of life.

— A. J. Cronin

Note to Self
Living Within Your Harvest

THE IDEAL – LIVING WITHIN YOUR HARVEST
Most of us associate *harvest* with gathering food from the land, but the ideal of living within your harvest is one that asks us to actually breathe, thrive, invest time interacting and connecting with those whom we come in contact every day. Living within your harvest means expressing compassionate love and concern for our fellow humans in the communities in which we live.

THE LOOK BACK
Describe an altruistic act you either witnessed or of which you were a part.

Why do you think this act has stayed in your memory? What was it that moved you?

THE INVITATION
When is the last time you recognized yourself giving?

Did it cause anyone else to also give?

Where was the place, your state of mind and time in your life that this occurred?

A BLESSBACK COURSE OF ACTION
What company, employee, news reporter, columnist, author or person of influence who has exhibited altruism would you thank if you had five minutes to do so?

Why do you want to thank them?

Will you write a BlessBack to that person, company, or organization?

BENEDICTION

It's easy to stay on my own plot of land,
but I know connecting means being relational.
Help me to BlessBack within my harvest.
Help me to see beauty in the ashes,
the heroes and she-roes in the dailies of life,
and to offer a spade of good words or actions their way.
I want to be a person of "because."

One drop of water
helps to swell the ocean.

— Hannah Moore
Notes From a Traveler Afar

CHAPTER SEVEN

BlessBacks Build A Better World

The charming and true-story, *84, Charing Cross Road*, is a compilation of letters between Helene Hanff and Frank Doel. Hanff was a writer and burgeoning playwright in New York City in the 1940s and '50s, frustrated with the lack of obscure British titles and the expense of quality books printed in the United States. She learned of a London bookstore that sold antique books and sent them her list of needs. Fulfilling the request fell to Frank Doel, Marks & Company's buyer.

Hanff and Doel's twenty-year correspondence began in 1949, where rationing was still a part of everyday life in England. When Hanff learned the British were allowed only two ounces of meat per family a week, she sent them a care package. Here is Doel's response:

20th December, 1949

Miss Helene Hanff
14 East 95th Street
New York 28, New York
U. S. A.

Dear Miss Hanff,
Just a note to let you know that your gift parcel arrived safely today and the contents have been shared … I should just like to add that everything in the parcel was something that we either never see or can only be had through the black market. It was extremely kind and generous of you to think of us in this way and we are all extremely grateful.

We all wish to express our thanks and send our greetings and best wishes for 1950.
                    Yours faithfully, Frank Doel
                    For MARKS & CO.[1]

Hanff continued sending the bookstore tins of food including ham and eggs. As the story unfolds, a friendship blooms, all because Hanff learned of England's limited food supply, and until the rationing ended, responded with her heart using the resources available to her. Though Hanff and Doel never met, Hanff not only bettered Doel's life but her food gifts provided the little world of people at Marks & Company not only protein and treats but a "We're in this with you" mentality while their country rebuilt after the war.

About ten years ago, my family went to work on a mission project in the hills of West Virginia. Philippi was a different world than mine. They ate turtle meat and "slaw;" they worked in mines and suffered from black lung. Many of the young women there — one was fourteen when she had married — had sixty-year-old husbands. Yet we worked together to fix the plumbing in the poorest of mobile homes and to repaint a church and its steeple.

When the team returned in the evenings to the college dorm that served as our home that week, all the volunteers gathered for dinner. But before we could eat, we each had to write on two index cards. No one was excused unless a person couldn't write. Each card had to name someone whom we "caught doing good" that day, and to say thanks. The process, having to write two cards about something good that happened in another, forced us to have an optimistic outlook on the day.

We called them our Barney cards, named after Barnabas (which means *encourager* in Greek). Barnabas visited the world's first Christian churches, noticing how other people cared for each other and telling them so.

Certainly being in an environment away from life's normal hustle and bustle made focusing and writing the cards each day easier to do; so did knowing we had to write two Barney cards to eat. The first time I saw my name on a card laying on the table set aside for them, I was surprised. I hadn't done any work that day that was different in purpose than the others. What had someone observed? When I flipped the card, I read, "I saw you sitting, visiting with Virginia today."

I had talked with Virginia, the pastor's wife, while taking a break from painting in the July heat of the day. How was that being "caught doing good"?

Whoever wrote that Barney card understood that part of building a better world is not just about physical labor. "There can be no community without communication," wrote Gilbert Bilezikian in *Community 101*. As Virginia and I visited that day, we built bridges to each other's worlds by learning about one another and conversing with each other relationally.

Working with and learning about the folks in West Virginia, along with writing BlessBack Barneys, created this little society of goodness. It kept the focus on other people, not on the work we each did. The good in our projects was measured not just by the size of one's talent or age but by living in a Barney state-of-mind, where encouraging one another was the standard. Little bits of gratefulness were everywhere and the more we looked for them, the more goodness seemed to expand and our worlds connected.

On the last afternoon of our trip, a church invited us to a picnic. Virginia had organized the meal. I thanked her for all the work she had done. "This wasn't work," she said in her accented English, "This was my *pleasure*." Her efforts were not seen as duty but as a way to build connections to my world and from it, she derived joy. She was made happy by having a serving heart.

LITTLE HOPES

Mother Teresa said, "I don't do big things. I do little things with big love." It's the little acts, the little hopes, on which we build up each other. And in life's truly difficult times, they can help us rebuild our lives.

Viktor Frankl in *Man's Search for Meaning* tells about his internment in a concentration camp in World War II. Morale had disintegrated when sicknesses and suicides rose to an alarming rate in a two-day span.[2] The block warden, sensing hopelessness throughout the camp, asked Frankl to talk to the prisoners. Though Frankl did not want to comply with anything the man said to him, he realized he had an opportunity to help his exhausted, starving, and nearly frozen companions in their darkest hour.

That evening, as the men lay in their earthen hut, the hut's only light bulb suddenly went out. In the darkness, Frankl talked quietly about their tragic and "irreplaceable losses," but that because they were alive, they still had hope. Life's tangible things — money, prestige, happiness and health were still a future possibility, he reminded the men. He offered them his favorite Nietzsche quote: "That which does not kill me, makes me stronger."

Frankl spoke of "little hopes" in the camp, such as being assigned an easier work load. Past joys, accomplishments, thoughts, dreams and even past suffering added up to living a significant life, he said. "What you have experienced, no power on earth can take from you." As men lay in their bunks, starving and frozen, Frankl continued, "Human life, under any circumstances, never ceases to have a meaning ... the hopelessness of our struggle [does] not detract from [life's] dignity and meaning."

When he finished, the light bulb coincidentally came on again. Men, in tears, hobbled to Frankl to thank him.

A breadth from death's door, courage came to these men when Frankl reminded them to remember who they once were and what they could still live to be. When they realized their every breath held significance and meaning, a will to live and thoughts of freedom rose, sustaining and helping them to endure.

Frankl's words gave little hopes, but another aspect about this story is that he said "yes" when given the opportunity, even when the opportunity came through the block warden, a man he despised.

In *The Psychology of Gratitude*, Robert Solomon, former professor of philosophy at the University of Texas-Austin, said cultivating gratitude "may come to define a good deal of one's character and one's sense of one's own life."[3] This is what naturally occurred in Frankl's life; he was tortured and near what felt like life's last breath, yet when called upon to bring hope to others, he put aside feelings about the warden and his own frail condition. He cultivated what hope he could and he did it by encouraging the men to remember the good — blessings, accomplishments and full lives —in their past and reminded them that they could have life again if they would struggle through each day using one little ray of hope to sustain them. In a sense, Frankl saved his community, and that community was his entire world.

We let our differences — the color of our skin, the language we speak, our religion, viewpoints, our politics, even our food choices — divide us. Yet we have so much to learn, give and receive from each other. If we step back and observe for a moment, we'll see where we connect. We're all human. We have physical, spiritual and emotional needs and desires. Each country, each community, each family and person has its struggles;

they may vary, but they nonetheless exist. We have hopes and dreams. We desire to survive each day.

Most important of all? We each have words for "love" in our languages. What would the world look like if we acted on that one word, for humanity's sake? For an answer, we can look to approximately 9,000 inhabitants on the plateau Vivarais-Lignon in south-central France. These people, acting individually, doing what came naturally to them and without consulting one another, saved an estimated 5,000 refugees during World War II, of whom were an estimated 3,500 Jews — many of them children.

How Goodness Happened

While taking an ethics course at the University of St. Thomas in the spring of 2008, we focused on what happened in Hitler's Germany. My professor, Rosemary Lemmons, assigned us readings such as John Stuart Mill, Thomas Aquinas and Ayn Rand to help us understand.

One reading, by Philip Hallie, in particular, affected me. Hallie was a professor of philosophy at Wesleyan University. Troubled by the evil of which humans are capable, Hallie wondered if goodness could be found. Hallie asked the question: Was there no good, simply for goodness' sake?

At the time Hallie posed his question in the 1970s, researchers had just begun to explore the behavior of the Vichy government and resistance efforts during Hitler's regime. Hallie's search resulted in his book, *Lest Innocent Blood be Shed: The Story of the Village of Le Chambon and How Goodness Happened There*. Hallie found goodness, in the most beautiful way, and it healed his soul.

Villages and hamlets dot the landscape on the Vivarais-Lignon plateau, a half-mile in the sky in the Haute-Loire department of France. Before the war, the charm of the plateau brought family tourists. The pretty countryside could be compared to Vermont. One could pick mushrooms and blueberries. One could fish in the Lignon river for trout and crayfish. An infinite number of walks could be taken along the river, by the thick pine forests, or around the extinct volcanoes le Lizieux and le Mézenc. People visiting stayed in apartments, small hotels and boardinghouses which later ironically, provided the structure that sheltered refugees.[4] Patrick Henry, professor emeritus of philosophy and literature at Whitman College, wrote *We Only Know Men: The Rescue of Jews in France*

101

during the Holocaust both to clarify some of Hallie's inaccuracies (they were colleagues), and to properly attribute the entire plateau as being a region that rescued and sheltered refugees.[5]

Thousands who helped on the plateau include thirteen local Protestant ministers and members of their parishes, Darbyites, Catholics, Evangelicals, the Salvation Army, farmers, shopkeepers, policemen, atheists with humanistic ideals, students, as well as those who worked in the underground railroad, and city dwellers who were themselves refugees. Others who aided were organizations such as Oeuvre de Secours aux Enfants (a Jewish children's rescue network), CIMADE (a joint committee of Protestant organizations to help refugees), the YMCA, Secours Suisse aux Enfants, American Quakers and the Boy Scouts.[6]

"To a large degree, it was an ecumenical effort uniting Protestants, Catholics of many denominations, and Jews in a collective struggle against a powerful common enemy," Henry wrote. "No similar ecumenical endeavor has ever been undertaken on French soil."[7]

At about the time I read Hallie's book, coincidentally I met Nelly Trocmé Hewett at a neighborhood book club. She shared her story of living as a young girl during the Nazi-occupied years in Le Chambon-sur-Lignon, a village on the plateau. Nelly's parents, André and Magna Trocmé, were deeply involved in the rescuing and sheltering of refugees — about seventy percent of whom were Jewish and children — from 1939 to 1945.

André's father was half-French, half-German and a Huguenot. His family accepted the "new faith" during the Reformation. He became a pacifist as a teenager. When German officers requisitioned part of his parents' large home, André found it strange that one of them did not carry a weapon and asked him why. The officer told him that he did not believe in killing but rather was fulfilling his service on the front line as a radio operator because he refused to carry a weapon.[8]

After graduating from the Paris Protestant Theological University, André went to Union Theological School in New York City in 1925 on scholarship. He met Magna Grilli di Cortona, a striking young Italian. Magna was also in the United States studying under scholarship at the New York School of Social Work. Magna descended from small Florentine nobility and Russian Decembrists. Thanks to her Russian grandmother, Varia Poggio Wissotzky, thoughts of service to others was always part of her life. André and Magna fell in love and became engaged within six weeks after their meeting.[9]

Because of his pacifist stand (which was illegal in France at the time), the only option before André, which he took in 1934, was to pastor a Protestant church in Le Chambon-sur-Lignon. Little did the church administration know that they had put the right man in the right place in the right time in history.[10]

Though France is predominantly Catholic, Chambon is an enclave of Huguenots, a deeply pious and religious population who live close to its values. The Huguenots are no strangers to persecution. They fled from their own persecution by the Roman Catholic Church three hundred years before to northern Italy, Germany, Sweden, England, and the United States. Some went to isolated areas in France — the plateau being one of them. Le Chambon had a tradition of welcoming strangers that extended as far back as the French Revolution when they hid some Catholic priests.

Welcoming was so embedded in the area that when Pastor Trocmé asked members of his church whether they would welcome children taken out of internment camps in southern France, his parishioners agreed. Though dangerous, residents housed exiled Jews and refugees, with new arrivals coming by the little narrow gauge railroad or bus.[11]

Marie Brottes, interviewed by Pierre Sauvage in *Weapons of the Spirit*, his award-winning documentary about the rescuing and sheltering that took place on the plateau, tells how during a Sunday service Brottes' pastor said, "Three Old Testaments have arrived." "We knew," she said, "that 'Old Testament' meant Jew. An old Christian got up and said, 'I'll take them,' and he brought them to his farm in the meadow and hid them."[12]

French police interviewed André and asked him to give the names of Jews who he knew were hiding in the area. "We don't know what a Jew is," André said. "We only know human beings."[13] The police, before leaving, warned him that his not answering could lead to his arrest in the future.

Journalists have asked those on Le Plateau Vivarais-Lignon why they protected foreigners of a different religion. "Because we had to help them," they said.[14] "It was the human thing to do," said Roger Darcissac, who hid refugees.[15]

Sauvage, the filmmaker, along with his parents, was sheltered on the plateau. He learned to walk in the barn on Henri and Emma Héritier's farm near Le Chambon. "The Protestant temples of the area and their pastors all played key roles in what happened here," Sauvage said. "But throughout the plateau and Le Chambon itself, the conspiracy of goodness that developed was, in important respects, both individualistic and unspoken. It was, above all, a matter of its only conscience."[16]

Daniel Trocmé, a second cousin to André, was director of Les Grillons, a home for children, and La Maison des Roches, a residence for male young adults in Chambon. Twenty months before he was arrested at La Maison des Roches and put to death in Majdanek concentration camp, Daniel wrote his parents on September 11, 1942. "For me, Le Chambon represents . . . a kind of contribution to the reconstruction of our world ..." he said. "I have chosen this adventure, not because it is an adventure, but so that I would not be ashamed of myself."[17]

In *Stories of Deliverance: Speaking with Men and Women Who Rescued Jews from the Holocaust*, Marek Halter tells villager Christian Algreen-Petersen's point of view. "We ... owe a debt of gratitude to the Jews for the task we were given and for the opportunity which they offered us in being able to help them: they obliged us, by letting us save them, and in so doing, safeguarded our self-respect."[18]

In Hallie's newest edition of *Lest Innocent Blood be Shed*, he tells the story of giving a lecture for the United Jewish Appeal. After talking about his book and Le Chambon, Hallie took questions. A woman in the back of the room asked Hallie if the Chambon he had written about was Le Chambon-sur-Lignon in Haute-Loire.

He said in his foreword, "Yes, this is the region."

The woman "seemed to crumble," Hallie wrote. "She said, 'You have been speaking about the village that sheltered my two daughters.'"

Her words silenced the room.

She walked to the front, near Hallie. "The Holocaust was storm, lightning, thunder, wind, rain, yes," she said. "And Le Chambon was the rainbow."[19]

William Hurlbut, physician and consulting professor at the Neuroscience Institute at Stanford, wrote that altruism is "unselfish action directed toward the welfare of others."[20] The plateau people lived altruism's very definition. Their powerful connection with another country's peoples was built on remembering how their own ancestors were persecuted centuries ago. They risked their lives to house others who were persecuted so they could live.

"Goodness requires a full measure of sacrifice," wrote P. Read Montague and Pearl H. Chiu in the February 2007 *Nature Neuroscience* journal.[21]

A group of Jews who had received shelter on the plateau placed a plaque across from the Protestant church in Chambon to honor the plateau's people. "Praise to the Protestant community of this Cévenol land and to all those led by its example, believers of all faiths and non-believers who, from 1939 to 1945, uniting together against the crimes of the Nazis, at the risk of their lives, during the Occupation, hid, protected, and saved thousands of those persecuted."[22]

Sixty-four years after the Liberation, French president Jacque Chirac chose Le Chambon-sur-Lignon from which to deliver a speech about the perils of racism. He praised the plateau for being "the moral conscience of [the] country."[23]

Francis Valla, Le Chambon's mayor welcomed the president saying, "Our country ... needs some beacons in the night. Your presence at our side today is a way of telling us that the plateau Vivarais-Lignon might be one of those beacons.[24]

In his preface to *Stories*, Marek wrote, "In paying homage to these Just Men and Women, in bringing to light their evidence, long kept in silence, I have tried to create a 'Memory of Good.' For Good is hope. And without hope one cannot live."[25]

We can make an emotional or mental picture of how we imagine a kind world would be. We can consciously look back at someone's good and carry that torch of memory into the future. Looking back at Vivarais-Lignon, we glimpse how active goodness extinguished evil. Hearing how one society valued another's right to live guides us in how we, as individuals, as a community, as a world, want to walk into our future.

Lesley Maber, a British woman who moved to Le Chambon before the war and taught school there for thirty years, believed that the people on the plateau were not necessarily exceptional, but that when people are faced with challenges in certain situations, they can come together to do good to one another for goodness' sake.

"Humanity is fundamentally good with the possibility to become fundamentally bad," Maber said. "And it's a choice. It doesn't mean that bad people are all bad and good people are all good. It doesn't mean that in Le Chambon there are no people with faults and failings. It's a community like any other community. And I think that means that any community anywhere has the choice to make and can choose right. People who seem very ordinary can do great things if they are given the opportunity."[26]

As the population of ministers and thousands of residents on a mountain in south-central France did, we can use "weapons of the Spirit"[27] to bring about what Magna called "a conspiracy of goodness"[28] in our cities, towns and villages. We can be active in our goodwill; we can intentionally live out kindness and goodness to others. By doing BlessBacks of our own, we rescue and give hope, and invest in the creation of that better world.

> *...be gentle and polite to all people.*
> — Paul's letter to a friend, Titus 3:2

I have a friend Lynn Rhinevault who comes to my house to garden. She is good at gardening and I am halfway decent at painting rooms. She clears the weeds and plants my flowers; I go to her house and paint a room purple, a dining room green. We complement each other.

One day as I sat next to her as she created a space for daffodils, she said, "I like to think that we are mending the broken sides of each other's fences. When my side starts to crumble, you come with your brick and mortar and mend my side; when your side starts to look shabby, I wet a spade and fill the gaps."

Psychologist Robert Solomon said humans tend to act as if they have gotten to where they are in life by themselves. We like to think our success is our own doing. It is only when we fail do we assign blame, he wrote in *The Psychology of Gratitude*.[29]

While much of what we do we accomplish through our own personalities and drive, the truth is, we are shaped by others who teach and help us develop into who we will become. Every meaningful person in our lives is part of its tapestry. Even our existence is not self-made.

We exist because someone gave us life. We achieve our purpose in life through family systems, beliefs, and experiences, all of which come to us through interacting with others. Because of others, our lives take on meaning.

Experience is never at bargain price.

— Alice B. Toklas

Fred "Hargy" Hargesheimer had no idea that when he was shot out of the sky on June 5, 1943 by a Japanese pilot it would alter his life's meaning and purpose.[30]

Fred was a twenty-seven-year-old American army lieutenant during World War II, and that Saturday had been a productive day of photo reconnaissance along the 370-mile coastline of Japanese-occupied New Britain, New Guinea in the Bismarck Sea. Despite the thick cloud cover, he spotted villagers in a canoe and tipped the left wing of his P-39 to nod a greeting. He headed east toward Cape Gloucester to take pictures of the enemy-occupied airstrip that American forces planned to capture by year's end. He saw Lolobau Island and spied the rumored hotspot where the Japanese hid their barges.

The sky suddenly cleared and at 8,000 feet, Fred knew his plane was exposed. He began a quick ascent and headed back to base at Dobodura, still in Australian territory.

Rat-ta-ta-tat. Rat-ta-ta-tat.

A saw-toothed rip appeared on the cowling of his left engine. Black smoke poured out. His right engine died. The pressure-gauge needle slumped to zero. He touched his wet forehead. Blood. Losing altitude fast, he pulled the emergency release lever, but the cockpit canopy only half opened. He unbuckled his seat belt and reached to jiggle the canopy loose.

Whoosh. Suddenly he was out of the plane and his parachute opened.

He steered his chute away from his downed plane to make it harder for the enemy to find him in the thick jungle. He landed halfway down the 4,000-foot Nakanai Mountains. He remembered he had a survival kit in his pack and among the findings were ten matches, extra ammo for his pistol, a small machete and two chocolate bars. He cut strips from his parachute to bandage the cut on his head and wipe the blood from his face and neck. He checked his compass and began to fight through a pathless jungle toward mainland New Guinea.

For ten days, he contended with an earthly mess of gushing rivers, rains that deluged, crocodile-filled rivers, and bugs the size of baseballs that wanted any piece of him he couldn't defend. His diet was a square of chocolate a day.

A man does battle with himself when he is alone and Fred was no exception. He thought of his family, his three brothers, his love of flying; he worried about encountering the enemy. To get him through he recited the twenty-third Psalm. He remembered learning that God helps those who help themselves.

On the eleventh day, he found a small abandoned grass hut. He used his last match, lit a fire, and lived on snails he found along the riverbed. When indigenous villagers found him, it was Day 31. Immediately they eased his fears and showed him a note an Australian officer had written: the locals were safe people and had helped other downed pilots.

For six months, the villagers provided food and shelter. Trust was reciprocal. They called him "Masta Predi" *Mister Freddie* and found a way to communicate using Pidgen English. Numerous times they led him to safety in the jungle when Japanese soldiers came through the village looking for him. When he contracted malaria, Ida, a young mother with a newborn son, produced an extra cup of milk a day and gave it to Fred until he was healthy again.

Fred received word through a pathway of interconnected natives of a planned rescue if he could get to the location thirteen miles away. He hurriedly said good-bye to the village that had saved his life. Through jungle, torrential rains and sliding ravines, Fred Hargesheimer, reached the coast on February 6, 1944. For three months Fred stayed with the coastwatchers — Australian commandos who risked their lives every day helping the Allies behind enemy lines — before his escape on a US submarine.

Life happened at warp speed once he was stateside. Fred married Dorothy and became a major in the army. Shortly thereafter, he decided upon a civilian life and the young couple moved to Minnesota to raise their three children.

But for sixteen years, the memory of the villagers and what they had done for him was front and center in Fred's mind; he never forgot their kindness. He wondered how he could ever repay his friends at Ea Ea, especially Luluai Lauo, and the native chief Joseph Gabu, who had hidden him more than once, and Ida, the nursing mother who helped him recover from malaria.

Fred's family gave up their vacation in 1960 so he could buy the $1,800 plane tickets and make the 10,000-mile trek back to thank the villagers.

Word had reached the villagers through Australians still doing reconnaissance in the area that Fred was coming to see them. In fact, they had expected him four days earlier. Fred arrived in moonlight. Villagers dressed in their Sunday best honored him by singing "God Save the Queen" as he disembarked from his boat. Luluai Lauo and Joseph Gabu both shook his hand. He found Ida and thanked her again for her life-saving milk. Her son was now sixteen.

Fred came home, overwhelmed at being reunited with the villagers who had saved him but still was not satisfied. "Back home, I wondered how I could repay the huge debt I owed to the friends who had saved my life," he said in his autobiography *The School That Fell From the Sky*. A New Guinea missionary home on furlough suggested he build a school.

For three years, Fred collected small donations. Five bucks here, a dollar there and in 1963 he returned with his son, Dick, and $15,000. Together they worked to create a school in Ewasse, near Ea Ea (now named Nantabu). They transported sand for the cement, eventually clearing a road with the Meramera (formerly Ea Ea natives) and hired a contractor to build the first permanent elementary school. The school had four classrooms. Fred hired four locals from New Guinea and an Australian headmaster. With help from American volunteers, in March 1964, the Airmen's Memorial School opened. The forty pupils ranged from first to sixth grade.

Once home, Fred continued to send funds, adding a library and more classrooms. In 1971, Fred secured a year's leave of absence with his employer so he, along with his wife, could, as Fred wrote, "say thank you in a meaningful way." Fred and Dorothy stayed four years, teaching and helping in any way they could.

More than five hundred students had attended the school by 1996. Today its graduates include attorneys and nurses. Three former students returned to teach at the school. In 2000, the village gave Fred the title "Suara Auru" meaning "Chief Warrior."

He made his last visit, one of nine, in 2006. He was ninety. The village had made many changes since 1963. People lived in concrete block houses rather than grass huts and had cell phones. Industry had arrived, due to discovery of oil palm near Lake "Hargy."

Garua Peni, a former student, holds a master's degree in linguistics from the University of Sydney and teaches at the University of Papua New Guinea. She said in the foreword to Fred's book:

"Whenever I count my blessings, I count the blessing of my friendship with Suara Auru Fred Hargesheimer and the Airmen's Memorial School in Ewasse ten times … Learning of a world outside my small village, exposure to other cultures, learning English, having a career, academic potential … for as long as I live, I will be grateful to have been a student at the Airmen's Memorial School in Ewasse."

The tiny village of Bialla, Papua, New Guinea may seem a strange place for a person to do a BlessBack, but for Fred Hargesheimer, those who lived there had never left his heart. Together, an airman and a village reciprocated their gratitude. As Fred said at the end of his book, "[It] was the people who kept bringing me back. I had found my purpose in life."

Fred's story is powerful, not only because it shows the possibilities and opportunities given to change the lives of others but also how we change ourselves through the exercise of a BlessBack. It's as if something gets in our blood and we cannot go back to the way we lived life before; we work to fulfill our purpose until the world we see in our hearts is the world we helped create.

Precious things have been put into our hands,
and to do nothing to honor them is to do great harm.

— Marilynne Robinson

A LIFE, SATISFIED

Sue, a fellow 88th Street Pussycat, called at 8:30 one night to tell me that her mom's days were numbered. Her phone call disturbed me. I knew Barb had been in the hospital and that the doctors couldn't pinpoint what was wrong. I hadn't expected to hear that she had days to live. That night I lay in bed and thought about my last visit with Barb and her husband Ted, two weeks ago.

Rick and I had walked into their house, down two doors from where

I grew up and where my mom still lives. My heart warmed with sweet memories of my childhood. The house inside was like a huge time capsule or a cocoon, just like the house I grew up in. Inhaling its aroma felt like taking a cleansing breath, meant to slow you down and focus in the moment.

The copper clock on the wall above the kitchen table still kept perfect time, as it had for fifty years. Marble-sized black and red balls showed the hours, reminding me of how we shape our lives around chronos time — "earth" time.

Soon Barb would change time zones and live permanently in God's time or kairos time. I felt selfish, not wanting her to leave.

But I am not the clock keeper for chronos time and must make the most of what will be my last visit with Barb. Each of us has, each day, the gift of time.

Barb's gray hair was curled and she wore a fluffy pink terry bathrobe as we sat on the couch. She saw me look at the glass on the end table next to her. The little girl in me wished the glass held watered-down chocolate milk instead of Ensure. I asked her how she was doing; Barb got right to the point. "I've lived a full life, Julie. I'm ready to go to Heaven. But I know it will be hard for everyone I leave behind."

We have a face we never show anyone and we have a face we show the world. I have no idea of Barb's last moment, but her gift of moments to me and her contented state reminded me of "satisfied." *Satisfy*, satis for enough, facere for *to do*. To do enough or enough to do. Either way, its meaning speaks of Barb's life. To fill, to meet expectation of. Here in chronos time, she had done enough.

In the historical account of Jesus visiting Martha's home in Luke, chapter 10, Martha was in the kitchen making a seven-course meal for her sixteen guests while her sister Mary sat near Jesus and feasted on His every word. Martha was frustrated because she was doing all the work. Verse 10:42 records Jesus saying to Martha, "Only one thing is needed." Though the main meaning is that Mary did what would last — she created memories of time spent with her Savior —another meaning exists here: We can overdo busyness in chronos time.

At a recent women's retreat, the speaker broke down the word *busyness*. Two characters in the Chinese language form the word: "kill" and "soul." *Killsoul* can so easily take control of our lives, but only if we let it. What emanated from Barb was serenity and contentment; she lived life, satisfied.

Eleanor Roosevelt's mother-in-law told a story about times when Eleanor's children would race into the house — late, of course. The kids made the excuse, "We didn't have time …" to which Eleanor's mother-in-law replied, "You had all the time there was."[30]

Barb's remaining time was to receive visitors and to say good-bye to them, and for them to be able to say what they needed to in their good-byes, too. That day, Barb gave me so much more. She taught me a lesson just by being in her presence and seeing the things she had intentionally kept the same in her house. The lesson was to live a satisfied life.

Every day is an event, yet the years seem to run together. Time, as we age, seems to escape from our fingertips. Life is filled with mandates. We wake up with a list of to-dos. What makes life bearable is that within its daily constraints, living the BlessBack life gives a person wiggle room in one's choices. It gives us freedom to live a life, satisfied.

At the end of the day, so the British cliché goes, life really is about how you spend it and with whom you allow to fill, change and bless your life. It's about the person who helped you re-discover life or re-conceive it. It's about the man or woman who reminded you that *killsoul* is not the focus of life. It's about being with great listeners, the ones who treat our words — the ones we say and the ones we don't — as priceless perfume, not to be wasted. It's about being with people, who when you are around them, make you think, "I breathe deeply here." It's about expressing your thanks to people in a way that, after you leave their presence, the scent of your thanks lingers so their lives are changed and they go on to change other lives with the BlessBack message.

Step into the time that remains and change the world.

Begin each day like it was on purpose.

— Alex "Hitch" Hitchens

Note to Self
Conspiracy of Goodness

THE IDEAL – CONSPIRACY OF GOODNESS

The conspiracy of goodness ideal is an intentional mindset in which to live, meant to fulfill another's need with gratitude. It's living each day honoring the humanity of another. It's doing goodness, for goodness' sake. It's about "safeguarding our self-respect," as Christian Algreen-Petersen said earlier. It's painting rooms and mending fences. "What kind of world do you want," penned Ben Harper of Ben Folds Five. "History starts now."

THE LOOK BACK

At different times, we serve different roles. We may be teaching a class one day and sitting listening the next. As you read Viktor Frankl's story of little hopes, were you standing with Frankl, echoing his words or were you internalizing his message and letting him speak hope, as the prisoners were, to you, too?

What are the little hopes you think of from your past? That you have for your future?

The Invitation

If you read the comments section of online news articles, you know the political climate in the United States seems filled with anger and tension. How can you be a part of a climate change that has to do with the atmosphere of Earth's residents?

If "Huguenot" and "Jew" was replaced with say, Democrat, Republican, Socialist, Christian, Muslim or Hindu, would you open your door and take them in if they were in need?

Do you know someone who has a different view than you do that causes tension in your interactions? What could you give him or her that would deflate that tension?

A BlessBack Course of Action

The Barney cards passed around the dinner table in West Virginia were in fact daily BlessBacks. Their intent was to remind us that in order to eat, one had to first look for and find goodness in others and thank them for it.

Before you eat your next meal, on two index-sized cards, give a Barney thank-you to two people for what they did today. The thanks need only be one sentence long, but the cards must each state why *today* you are thankful for the person. Deliver the note, whether you place it on someone's desk or send it inter-office mail, use your mail carrier, or hand it to a stranger as you walk by. Whether you stay anonymous or you let yourself be known is up to you.

BlessBack Barneys. Go, change the world as only you can do.

BENEDICTION

Help me see
where I need to thank those who have repaired my fences.
May I act today
to inflate and deflate, as needed,
and if necessary, to use a BlessBack Barney
to live in a conspiracy of goodness.
Help me use my gratitude
to create the world I wish to see.

Sacrifice is a positive act.
Its sense is something given; not something given up.

— Evelyn Underhill
Notes From a Traveler Afar

CHAPTER EIGHT

Why We Hesitate to Give BlessBacks

I know death hath ten thousand several doors
for men to take their exits.

— John Webster

People influence our lives, for good or for bad. When people hurl harsh words in our direction, sometimes the power of their words diminishes who we are becoming — sometimes momentarily, sometimes for years, sometimes for a lifetime. Those who diminish us are like the shifting tectonic plates mentioned in Chapter Three; when their words slam against us, they affect us, and our hearts submerge.

Marilyn Gartner is in her seventies but still remembers when her sixth grade teacher, Mrs. Paulson, asked students to draw a picture of their choosing. The winner, chosen by the class, was to receive a twenty-five-cent ticket to see The HMS *Pinafore* at the local theater. Marilyn drew a portrait of two curly-haired terriers and colored her drawing. The class declared Marilyn's picture the winner. Happy, Marilyn could barely sit still as her teacher walked to the front of the room. Instead of holding up Marilyn's drawing, Mrs. Paulson held up another student's drawing. "Here's my vote," she said, vetoing the students' choice and handing the theater ticket to another girl.

Marilyn recalls that day. "I was devastated. Mrs. Paulson unfairly changed the rules," she said. Later that day, Mrs. Paulson handed Marilyn a quarter so she could go to see the play. She didn't go. "Being given the money didn't feel the same."

Marilyn did not draw again until she had three children. One day she quickly drew animals on a sketch pad at the kitchen table. Her oldest daughter said to her, "You can really draw, Mom." Marilyn hid twenty years of artistic talent because she felt rejected and shamed by a teacher. Today, Marilyn must silence Mrs. Paulson's words of rejection each time she begins to draw.

When Claudia Sullivan was a child, she loved to sing. Her mother overheard her and told her not to sing in public because she thought Claudia had a terrible voice. Now, thirty-five years later, Claudia sits in the front pew in church so no one hears her sing.

When we are publicly or privately shamed, like Marilyn and Claudia, we experience what the French novelist and essayist Marcel Proust called "upheavals of thought." Our emotions mentally freeze the incident; our bodies flinch at the remembered upheaval. Long after the damaging event, we recall the words and the person's tone of voice who conveyed them. We submerge our souls because the words singed and stung. We hide parts of our character, or our talents for years. People speak their opinions, often without our solicitation of them, and before you know it, those opinions affect us, sometimes wounding us terribly. If we let the words sink in, they will stop us from going out into life.

Oprah Winfrey, in the September 2000 issue of *O* magazine, said when she was fourteen her father told her she was going to be overweight because her mother, aunt, and grandmother were. Her father altered Oprah's mental and physical landscape. She wrote that even as she won beauty pageants, helmed an iconic American talk show, and successfully ran a marathon, her father's comments undermined her success.[1]

When Giving a BlessBack Isn't What You Expected

When you give a BlessBack, you are risking yourself. You are putting yourself in somewhat of a vulnerable position. That someone may reject your BlessBack, or reject you, is a possibility.

Kyle Krieger sat in his tenth grade history class, thinking about how much he loved the subject. He realized he owed his interest in the subject to Mr. Peck, his eighth grade history teacher.

He came home and wrote a thank-you note to Mr. Peck. The next week his mom drove him to his old school so Kyle could deliver it.

As Kyle walked down the corridor, he was awash in memories, excited to see Mr. Peck again. He knocked on Mr. Peck's door. Mr. Peck was correcting papers.

"Hi, Mr. Peck. How are you?"

"I'm good. What can I do for you?"

Kyle hesitated. Why had he asked that? It couldn't be that uncommon for former students to come back and revisit their old school and teachers. Yet he continued to correct papers and not look at him. "I just came back to see you," Kyle said. He handed him his thank-you note. "I just wanted to stop in and say 'hi' and to say thanks for being a great teacher."

Mr. Peck looked at him with a blank stare and fumbled with the letter, leaving it unopened. "Oh, okay, well, thanks for coming by."

Sweat crept from Kyle's head to his neck. His hero didn't remember him. "Have a nice day. Nice to see you."

"Yeah, you, too."

Kyle got in the car.

"Wow, that was quick. How'd it go?" said his mother.

"Just get out of the parking lot, Mom. I don't ever want to come to this school again." Kyle said, working hard not to cry.

There's no getting around it. Not being remembered, not being seen as someone worth remembering, feels awful.

Like Kyle, I have experienced it.

I gave a BlessBack in my thirties to Wesley, a credit manager of an insurance company I worked at when I was nineteen. I went back with a friend who had been the receptionist, someone he'd hardly known, whereas he and I worked together every day. As the three of us sat in his office, he said, "I remember you, Margaret, but I don't remember you, Julie." I related every memory I had of us working together. "You really don't remember me?" I asked.

> *Is thanking someone from your past worth the risk of that person not remembering you? The answer is "yes."*

He just shrugged and said, "No, I'm sorry, but I don't."

At these times, life bursts our bubbles and good intentions are stomped to smithereens. We are disappointed and embarrassed by not being remembered.

Is thanking someone from your past worth the risk of that person not remembering you? The answer is "yes." However, I had to live the other side of receiving a BlessBack from someone I didn't remember to get to that viewpoint.

About ten years ago, I led the children's choir at my church. They were sixty squirrely, eight- to eleven-year-old, crazy-fun kids. The hour of choir practice was fast-paced. The pianist and I had to get through six or so songs, trying to get the kids to learn what harmony was, to learn the lines, the words, and to sit still in a small room. Some kids came every week, some once a month. No one ever sat in the same place twice.

A couple of years ago, the mom of one of the kids told me how much something I had said meant to her daughter.

I wish I could remember what I said, but I honestly don't. The daughter is the nicest girl. She's in college now and says "hi" to me when we see each other, but every time I see her, I feel terrible that I don't remember the incident that so affected her.

But as terrible as I feel, I am so glad to know I impacted her life.

After a particularly insightful conference on public speaking, Jean Rae wrote her instructor. Here's what she wrote:

> *Dear Terri,*
> *I have wanted to write this letter for weeks, but life's busyness seems to keep us from reacting when we should.*
>
> *When I graduated from your speaker conference in Boston ten years ago, I did not realize at the time the real value of what you were teaching and demonstrating. In retrospect, I see clearly now the advantage it presented and the opportunities it has brought me.*
>
> *My first big speaking gig was in front of 1,000 people at a leadership summit. After my presentation, someone came to me and said, "You are a polished speaker with some good training behind you."*
>
> *I will never forget that comment. At that instant, God brought to my mind you, the person behind it all, whom He raised up to teach me the things needed to impact lives, teach others, and instill hope.*

You gave me the tools and the confidence to achieve dreams I never thought possible. Today, I am speaking and writing in places I never dreamed I could.

My heart is grateful to you for impacting my life in a way I'll never forget.

Sincerely, Jean

Jean wrote her BlessBack five years ago. Jean's recipient has never acknowledged her BlessBack.

Not everyone will acknowledge your BlessBack, either. That's okay. You're in good company. Even the efforts of the apostle, Paul, went unacknowledged. He writes at the end of Philippians. "Not one church shared with me in the matter of giving and receiving, except you only … not that I am looking for a gift." Sometimes we must be satisfied with just the simple fact that we took the chance to express our gratitude.

Giving gratitude is not always going to go the way you want it to go. But to live without gratitude is to deny yourself the possibility of a surprising and wonderful life. This is how Joseph Stalin chose to live: denying himself and others the beauty found in giving and receiving gratitude.

Stalin was a paranoid dictator who led by intimidation, according to Nikolai Tolstoy in his book *Stalin's Secret War: a Startling Expose of his Crimes Against the Russian People*. He demanded three-inch thick windows in his vehicles, impenetrable even against machine-gun fire.[2] He had four hundred personal bodyguards and went to extreme measures to ensure his food was not poisoned.[3] Trusting no one, he tested his comrades' loyalties by inviting those under his command to dine with him. Guests could not predict the evening's outcome. Either he awarded them with honors, tested their pain tolerance by lighting their fingernails on fire, sent them to the Gulag or his mines, or shot them.[4]

He treated his family the same. His firstborn son Jakov served in the Red army. He was captured and sent to Sachsenhausen concentration camp near Berlin. When the Germans tried to negotiate Jakov's return to freedom in exchange for Russia's return of German prisoners of war, Stalin stalled the process, called Jakov, "my fool" because he thought his son showed weakness in character for agreeing to be swapped out from the camp. Upon hearing his father had abandoned him, Jakov walked into an electric fence.[5]

A comrade of Stalin's once asked the dictator if he understood gratitude. Stalin "took out his pipe...murmured reflectively and replied, 'Oh yes, I know; I know very well; it is a sickness suffered by dogs.'"[6]

Gratitude was a weakness in Stalin's eyes. He believed gratitude created dependency and "crippled dogs" — his term for his own people. He refused to think of gratitude as a virtue to nurture.

One can only guess where Stalin's disgust for gratitude originated. The late philosopher Robert Solomon believed ungratefulness was "a sign or symptom of lack of socialization. To deny the obvious truth [of our need of help from others] ... is not just to be philosophically mistaken. It is to be a person of poor character, whatever one's other virtues."[7]

Most of us do not hold Stalin's extreme views. But some of us are uncomfortable with giving and receiving gratitude. Some will even go to great lengths to avoid it.

THE TROUBLE WITH GRATITUDE

Maia Kimball is generous in giving gratitude but has a hard time accepting it. In 2009, when her mother died, she received more than one hundred sympathy cards from family, friends and acquaintances. The cards, hidden away in one of her mother's antique hat boxes, still remain unopened. Though Maia knows people wrote comforting words and gave memorial gifts, she has chosen to hide them. Receiving these gestures of sympathy feels wrong to her because opening the cards takes the focus away from her mother and puts it on her. She would just as soon weather the storm of grief on her own.

Maia's mindset, to not be indebted by gratitude, erases the love and concern expressed to her. Further, by her rejecting the sincerity of friends' altruist acts, she has become the center of attention with her donors; they don't understand her brush-off of their condolences and gift-giving. To them, she has rendered their thoughts as insincere and disingenuous.

Living a gratitude-filled life is not only an acknowledgement of debt and expression of humility, according to Solomon, but gratitude improves one's life.[8] This is what Maia dislikes — that she might benefit from another's giving. As a result, both the one grieving and those offering condolences have missed the beneficial exchange of blessing.

A BlessBack is a pleasure-filled gift, not something to lament receiving. Maia has missed the soul-to-soul meaning of a BlessBack, that others gave of themselves to honor her mother and her memory.

INSINCERE GRATITUDE

Insincere gratitude kills good gratitude. If we get a whiff of false appreciation, the next time we keep silent. This happens most times when relationships are lopsided, such as in hierarchical teacher/student, doctor/patient, or employer/employee relationships, and people take advantage of the relationship for monetary, economic, or social gain.

Insincere gratitude kills good gratitude.

Because we learn to judge sincerity at an early age, it doesn't take us long to sniff out someone's "agenda."

Vanessa Gunderson, a generous wealthy woman in a Texas suburb, was best friends with Chelsea McGuire, a fellow employee. The company where both women worked implemented a plan to reward employees for charitable fundraising. Chelsea began to host a monthly fundraiser for a charity close to her heart. Vanessa was an equal partner in the endeavor. Each month she brought three or four hors d'oeuvres to Chelsea's house. Soon Chelsea added to Vanessa's list of appetizers and asked Vanessa to bring a case of wine. Before long, every month Chelsea hosted and Vanessa spent hundreds of dollars in food and drinks.

The fundraisers were successful, but there can only be one winner. Six months later, Chelsea received a promotion for her fundraising efforts and dropped Vanessa's friendship. Vanessa learned her friend's motive was not to deepen their friendship but to climb the corporate ladder. Vanessa still volunteers, but because someone took advantage of her good heart, she no longer jumps in with both feet. She dips one careful toe in at a time.

Some of you, like Vanessa, may bear the mark of trauma and bad gratitude. Your heart is still genuine in your gift giving, but your betrayal by supposed friends stings. Unfortunately, journeying makes one susceptible to the elements. It's wise to be aware of reckless drivers, but don't let them stop you from venturing down the BlessBack road.

The same is true in relationships. These are the risks of the road. We must keep going because we will encounter good in the miles ahead, because we possess the ability to make it so. "True generosity consists precisely in fighting to destroy the causes which nourish false charity," wrote Paulo Freire. When you BlessBack, you beautify the world. Never let someone's betrayal or insincerity stop you from continuing on your gift-giving journey.

Never let someone's betrayal or insincerity stop you from continuing on your gift-giving journey.

GRATITUDE AND THE ZERO-SUM GAME

Perhaps you heard someone say, or have even thought to yourself, "I don't want to be invited to someone's home for dinner. If I do, I'll feel obligated to reciprocate." This happened to Jessie and John Geddes. They repeatedly invited a co-worker and his wife to dinner, but the answer was always, "no."

"We finally realized they kept declining because they felt they would have to have us back," Jessie said.

Just as we retreat from insincere gratitude, we can feel indebted to displays of kindness. Fear of feeling tied to the relationship, or worse, feeling obligated to reciprocate may also cause us to decline an invitation to interact.

Relationships are hard to decode. We presume and assume we know each other's views. Sometimes though, we get it wrong.

Renee Hawkins tried to befriend her co-worker, Cynthia Owens, and asked her the date of her birthday. "It's July 20th," Cynthia replied, "but don't get me a card because then I'll have to spend money on a card for you."

Upon hearing Cynthia's comment, Renee presumed Cynthia did not want to expand their acquaintance into a friendship. But Renee forged ahead and trusted her instincts that a wonderful person was behind Cynthia's barrier and continued to pursue a friendship with her. The friendship is now thirty years old and still going strong.

Sue O'Neill does not send out birthday cards for a different reason. "I'm afraid I'll slip up one year and forget someone's birthday and they will think I'm trying to signal that I want to end the friendship when it's nothing of the sort," she said. Instead, Sue blesses her friends in a unique way. "I send them cards or drop a gift by when I see something in a store that reminds me of a certain friend," she said. "I want them to know I thought of them when I saw the gift."

In *Our Mutual Friend*, indebted gratitude plays out in reverse:

Mr. Podsnap, says to his wife, "I think we should have some people [to dinner] on Georgiana's birthday."

Mrs. Podsnap's reply: "Which will enable us to clear off all those people who are due."

The Podsnaps invite those on their list, only to have all of them decline. Mrs. Podsnap's response is classic. "Asked, at any rate, and got rid of."[9] In this instance, the Podsnaps had a dinner party to remove the Podsnaps' weight of indebtedness. "Most people experience indebtedness as an unpleasant and aversive psychological state"[10] said psychologists who study the field of gratitude. Like the Podsnaps, feeling indebted by gratitude is like a sliver under our skin, annoying us until we extract it. We want the gratitude scorecard even, with no debt owed. "No other animal plays zero-sum games as tirelessly as we do," said Robert Wright in *Time* magazine.[11]

GRATITUDE'S OBLIGATORY ASPECT

We feel uncomfortable and the need to erase the unequal balance and achieve what Kristin Bonnie and Frans de Waal call "social reciprocity" because received gratitude feels like we should repay another's kindness.[12] How like humans to subliminally keep track of the invitational score. We feel better when we are on an even keel with each other, especially when accepting a courtesy from someone with whom we'd rather not be in a relationship.

Somehow, though not to Stalin's extent, we complicate gratitude.

We have gone from showing sincere thanks to keeping ugly gratitude tallies where injuries and isolation occur.

The past is a foreign country. They do things differently there.

— L. P. Hartley

Your act of blessing is not about people remembering you. It's about your remembering them — their expressions, their attitudes, and the way they lived their lives — in thankfulness.

The words, the actions that affected you — no one can take them away. They are real and deserve honor, even if the person whom you are honoring does not remember you or respond in a reciprocal way.

The point of a BlessBack is that it is a gift. That means no strings attached. No self-dampering allowed. Besides, there will be plenty of people who will be grateful for your being genuine and sincere in your thanks to them.

> *Your act of blessing is not about people remembering you. It's about your remembering them...*

When you receive a BlessBack, you learn you made a difference to a fellow human, but you also receive what C. S. Lewis called "the divine accolade." Receiving a BlessBack can feel childish in the most beautiful way, if you let it. A little bit of pureness is restored when we advance goodness, and receive goodness.

We can only be said to be alive in those moments
when our hearts are conscious of our treasures.

— Thornton Wilder

THE IDEAL – COASTLINERS

In this chapter, we have learned how we can damage each other with words and actions. We have learned how insincere gratitude and counting the gratitude score keeps us from the blessings found in giving and receiving BlessBacks.

THE LOOK BACK

Who is someone from your past who fits into the category of being a negative coastliner to you and why?

THE INVITATION

An examined life reveals your intentions, your missed opportunities, your course corrections and what you consider worthy of your time and effort to pursue. For this *Note to Self,* examine both kinds of coastliners in your life. What have they taught you about determination, resilience, surrender, boundaries?

A BLESSBACK COURSE OF ACTION

On vacation on Cadillac Mountain in Maine's spectacular Acadia National Park, Rick and I came upon cairns, little stacks of stones, which marked otherwise invisible trail paths on the giant boulders. They showed the way from where we'd come to where we were headed.

Last spring I created a timeline of my life. By the time I finished my life's contents, I had four sheets of paper taped together. The obvious cairns came first, family, marriage, children. But then I started to fill in the space between the markers with moments that mattered just to me and the people — teachers, friends, relatives, kids, and those whom I call "freighbors," all played a part in my journey. Creating a timeline forced me to look at the pivotal moments, the times I stepped back, and the restarts that helped me walk toward my dreams and goals. I fashioned this timeline to spotlight the pivotal moments in my mental, spiritual and physical life. I discovered some of my stops were merely rests and at the lowest points, God came closest and I grew the most spiritually.

Take a blank piece of paper and create a timeline. Put today's date and work backward. You don't have to use a straight line. You can shape it any way you like, whether you start in the center and work outward in rings or shape it like a snake with hills and valleys.

Mark the places where you have intentionally pulled away from someone who expressed gratitude to you. What were your reasons? Were they valid?

If not, how can you begin to embrace giving and receiving BlessBacks from those who are sincere?

Put the good times down and the times when life was hard on your timeline. What did you truly consider worthy of your time and effort to pursue, all of which made you the beautiful *you* you are today? When you have finished your project, step back and look for the times where you changed the most, based on the "cairns" who pointed the way. Write down their names here.

BENEDICTION

Guide me to the people who are coastliners I can trust.
As I have looked back over my life,
I realize just how significant people are to my own journey through life.
Some have only stayed for a year or two;
some have been with me since I was born.
Help me honor them in a way that reflects their impact
and my gratitude for their influence.

Let's build bridges here and there
Or sometimes, just a spiral stair ...
... oh, let's build bridges everywhere
and span the gulf of challenge there.

— Georgia Douglas Johnson
Notes From a Traveler Afar

CHAPTER NINE

When the Person You Want to BlessBack Has Memory Loss or Has Passed Away

Ah, when to the heart of man
Was it ever less than a treason
To go with the drift of things,
To yield with a grace to reason,
And bow and accept the end
Of a love or a season?

— Robert Frost

Kari Torejesen was born in 1925 and spent a good portion of her childhood in China, living with woman missionaries and parents who were part of Britain's suffragist movement. The women were strong, able in mind and body, to handle the harsh and dangerous life.

Later she met and married Robert Malcolm and they became missionaries to the Philippines. When they returned to the United States in 1974, Kari was shocked by what she was seeing and hearing within Christian homes.

The feminist movement was just beginning to explode. Some women wanted to take on a vocation outside of their home but felt that they would be abandoning their families. Yet, to Kari, the choice facing some Christian women who stayed at home seemed to her like a bizarre, nineteenth-century middle- and upper-class British view that required them to stay home and take care of the children and allow the husband to rule over their spiritual lives.

This troubled Kari. Allowing husbands to rule over their spiritual lives meant the women had replaced Christ with a human figure; they had assigned a human role meant for the Divine.

Kari wrote *Women at the Crossroads* in the late '70s to address these issues. She believed another option existed: walk straight ahead, in relationship with God. By going straight ahead with God at the helm, women could freely pick from either world.

Since the book's publication in 1974, thousands of women have read Kari's book. I am one of them. Not long ago, I went to express my thanks to her, but it was too late. She had Alzheimer's. I told her daughter how her mother's book was a big reason I became the person I am today. Kirsten said, "Will you tell my dad? You will encourage him."

Bob Malcolm and I had a great conversation. I told him what a remarkable woman Kari was and how she had shaped my life and that I had gone "straight ahead," using the gifts God had given me. He said, "So, you're one of them, too." He explained how more than twenty women had written him in the past two years to tell him that they were in women's ministry because of his wife's book and message.

Kari had wonderful visitors at the nursing home, Bob said, but that wasn't always the case for others. He had asked his two buddies, who also had dementia-suffering wives, if friends ever came to visit their wives in the nursing home. "Both of them said to me, 'We no longer exist among those people.' They were obviously wounded in their spirits," Bob said. "One of them burst into tears and said, 'I can understand that people don't know how to handle it when a person has dementia and the best way seems to be to disappear off the radar, but it would be nice if every once in a while some of my wife's colleagues would just stop in and be with us a little bit. They don't have to talk, just be with us.'"

Bob said the men would love it if someone from their past came to tell them why their wives were significant.

Bob's daughter said that her father was really comforted by hearing stories of Kari's influence in women's lives. "It helps Dad to remember what a gift to the world my mother was," Kirsten said.

If, in your search for your life influencers, you learn they have a condition such as Kari's, contact that person's loved ones and tell them your memories. You will encourage the caregivers and remind them of the way their loved ones once were.

OFFER COMPANIONSHIP

My father, Don Trewartha, reached the point with Alzheimer's disease where Carol, my mom, could not leave him alone. As his sole caregiver, Mom had times of great stress. A group of Dad's male friends wanted to help and show Dad how much they cared about him. They talked between themselves and offered Mom a once-a-week break. Mom used that time to run errands, go to lunch with a friend, and get some respite for herself. Though Dad didn't always understand why, he knew they were there. The men's visits supported their friend in his dark hours and helped Mom to caregive longer and better. Our family will never forget how they showed their thankfulness of having Dad as their friend in the way they did.

> *When you sit with someone you love who can't communicate with you anymore, you learn simple gestures express thanks.*

When you sit with someone you love who can't communicate with you anymore, you learn simple gestures express thanks. Sitting in silence with the person you love can be the most meaningful way to express a BlessBack to him or her.

WAITING TO SLEEP

Heidi Larkin's father, Bob Richter, had a rare brain disease similar to Alzheimer's. In the last year of his life, he could not communicate and his family was unsure of exactly how much he understood what was being said to him. For Bob's seventy-fourth birthday, the five Richter children and their spouses gathered around Bob's bedside at the nursing home where he lived. Each one expressed why he or she was grateful to their father. When they all had finished, they sang "Happy Birthday" to their dad. A tear slid down the side of Bob's face; they knew he understood.

A year later, the family gathered around his bedside once again, only this time their mom, Jean, Bob's wife of forty-nine years, was there. They shared and expressed their love and appreciation to Bob, both for who he was and for all he had done in their lives. Bob passed away shortly afterward. "It was like Bob was waiting to hear his children's blessings before he died," said Heidi's husband.

We are not always going to be on time, in an earthly way, in thanking those who've influenced us, but there are still meaningful ways to give our BlessBacks. Lissa Johnson found a beautiful way to honor the memory of her deceased grandmother.

Lissa grew up in Cleghorn, a tiny farming community in northwestern Iowa. Her grandmother, Anna Schuknecht, was a major life influencer for her. When Lissa was a little girl, her grandmother taught her bedtime prayers. When Lissa started confirmation, Grandma Anna gave her her first Bible. Lissa listened to her grandmother sing hymns in church and learned about God from her. But Lissa was shy when it came to expressing her thanks to her.

Lissa was married and had two children when Grandma Anna passed away in 1997. After the funeral and to Lissa's surprise, she learned her grandmother had bequeathed $1,000 to each grandchild.

Lissa's daughter, Lori, had recently expressed an interest in learning to play the piano so Lissa used her inheritance to buy her daughter a piano. Her daughter mastered the piano and majored in music. Lissa's thank-you to her grandmother was a forward BlessBack.

Today, the circle of Anna's blessing has widened. Anna taught Lissa how to worship God through music and Lissa's love of worshiping through music spread to her daughter; Lori is now a worship leader in a church. The circle of gratitude continues to expand: Lissa's two grandsons, Caleb and Ben, minister in their churches as well through guitar and drums.

Harriette Peoples also has found a simple and beautiful way to honor her friend who died five years ago.

I met Harriette in a food line at a cafeteria. She had on a stunning amethyst bracelet. "I bought that bracelet when my friend died," Harriette said. "She loved purple and I wear this to remind me of her and what a wonderful person she was in my life."

Harriette's idea of honoring her friend is an ongoing remembrance. It's a way to remember her friend by carrying her friend's memory with her in a tangible way.

Gayle Roper's husband, Chuck, passed away in the summer of 2010. To express their love, friends of the couple planted a tree in the yard of the church Gayle and Chuck helped to get started forty years ago. "The thoughtfulness of the group meant a lot to me as a sign of their regard and affection for Chuck and as a token of their support for me," Gayle said. "Knowing that Chuck is remembered is important to me. He truly was a great guy. Seeing the tree is a symbol of his evergreen life and spirit."

In my family, we've found a way to do this for my father.

My husband and I, along with our three sons and my brothers' families, celebrate Christmas every year in the house in which I grew up. Mom makes a delicious meal along with sandbakkels and krumkake for dessert from Norwegian recipes more than one hundred years old. When Dad passed away in July 2001 from Alzheimer's disease, Mom kept the holiday's traditions, but offered a new one. "Before we open gifts," she said. "I want us to go around the room and tell each other what we're thankful for." She gave us time to think about what we would say by taking the lead: "I am grateful for the forty-one years I had with your father."

Our expressions of gratitude were awkward and unoriginal at first, but as we went around the room, our contributions grew livelier. Some remembered Dad's groaners, like, "Let's make like a tree and leave," or the Woody Woodpecker call he mimicked perfectly. Some were just little when Dad's illness interrupted his life so they remembered him in the nursing home. "I liked that I got to take Grandpa around in his wheelchair," said one niece. We all expressed gratitude for Dad's influence in our lives.

That Christmas Day turned into a tender honoring of my father, discovering how each of us held something of Dad's unique personality in our memories. Mom's question caused us to pause, to measure the treasured gift of the person we had had the pleasure of knowing.

A RACE TO REMEMBER

Betty Liedtke didn't know her mom had breast cancer until after her mom died. It was 1971 and eighteen-year-old Betty had just started college. People did not discuss cancer as openly then as they do now and parents did whatever they could — as parents still do today — to shield their children from things that could hurt them.

Betty felt guilty for not knowing her mother had cancer, and she felt helpless and powerless because there was nothing she could do.

Years later, she felt helpless again when her sister Barb Veenstra was dying of pancreatic cancer. Her sister had gone from doctor to doctor, misdiagnosed each time. By the time they discovered what was wrong, she was dying. It was painful and frustrating to see Barb suffering physically and emotionally, only to lose her life from the awful disease.

A few months after losing Barb, Betty's youngest sister, Chris Hale, suggested on a return trip home from Chicago that the sisters do a cancer walk in honor of Barb and their mother. Soon after, Betty received a call asking if she would speak at the upcoming Eastern Carver County Relay for Life. She agreed and put a team together for the relay. Betty and her family, her father, her two sisters and families, came from around the country to hear Betty speak and to walk in the event.

Doing something in your loved one's honor is a beautiful, pro-active way to do a forward BlessBack for your missing loved one.

"It felt very empowering and validating to walk in the relay, and it also felt like an honoring and appropriate tribute to my mom and sister," Betty wrote. "It was all of us saying, 'We remember you. We miss you. We're honoring you by doing this, and we want the sacrifices you made (voluntary or not) to mean something to others and to help others who are fighting against cancer in their own lives.'"

As Betty walked the relay, she realized others around her also walked in memory or support of someone. "I was inspired, especially, by the high school students. They, too, had felt the pain and loss that cancer causes, and they took this very seriously. I was touched by the dedication and determination of all of them."

Betty said that taking part in the relay helped her to acknowledge those she'd lost and to remember how important they were to her. Their walk also raised funds to help others. "That makes us part of [my mom and sister's] legacy and it's a good feeling."

Betty and her family showed, by participating in a cancer walk, you can do something for those who died or who are sick. Doing something in your loved one's honor is a beautiful, pro-active way to do a forward BlessBack for your missing loved one.

Using the Memories of Loved Ones
to Empower You and Others

Thousands of children died of polio in the summer of 1946 in the United States. Sam came home from his pharmacist job in Minneapolis to find his eight-month-old son, Bob, with a spiked temperature and limp limbs. He cradled him in his arms and ran a mile and a half to a hospital where a Roman Catholic nun, Sister Kenny, treated polio victims with an unconventional method. Instead of the usual attempts with ice to cool the fever, Sister Kenny wrapped towels, as hot as patients could tolerate, around their limbs, to drive out the virus. Bob was one of twenty-two patients treated in the experimental program. His right arm, diaphragm, and legs recovered. Only his left arm suffered. Bob's father and Sister Kenny saved Bob's life.

"Growing up, Dad taught me how to fall so I would not hurt myself. He taught me how to protect myself if someone threw a punch at me," Bob said. "Dad told me physically I could do anything, yet emotionally Dad could not heal me or protect me from people when I was introduced to them and how they looked from my face to my shriveled arm. He could not protect me from kids picking on me."

What good had come from having polio, Bob often wondered. "I'd tell God, 'I know You could have kept this from me and not allowed it. Yet You didn't. Why?'"

Bob co-led a crusade in India in the late 1990s. While there, he learned that India has more than 400,000 villages, half without clean drinking water. He made several more trips there, learning about the culture and people. In 2007, Bob founded a non-profit organization, *Village to Village Ministries*, which funds annual crusades in India, assists in church plantings, and aids the tiny parishes by drilling freshwater wells for the villagers to use. Every six-hundred-dollar well that is bored has the potential to give water to a thousand villagers. Dozens of Indians experienced permanent healings at the crusades; Bob attributes the ministries' results all to God's power.

At times, Bob's courage falters. He wonders, at sixty-six, how a man from Minnesota, without a college degree and a shriveled left arm, leads crusades to thousands. "Every time I stand before the crowd and I start to doubt myself, my mind goes back to when I was a young boy standing at the edge of a pool, learning to swim. I see my father standing in the water below, stretching his arms to me. I hear his gentle voice. 'You can do it, Bob. Come on. You can do it. I know you can do it.'"

His father died in 1983.

"The mind is an enchanting thing … [i]t has memory's ear that can hear without having to hear … " wrote Marianne Moore.[1] Through Bob's "memory ear," his father's trustworthy love, which gave him the confidence to jump into a pool of water as a kid, now gives him the courage to go on stage and reach into the lives and hearts of Indian villagers.

While walking toward a village in January 2008, Bob saw a man sitting in the middle of a dirt road one hundred yards ahead of him. As Bob walked closer, the man hurriedly tried to drag himself off the road. He only had one working limb — his right arm. His other arm and both legs were shriveled and crippled.

"The mind is an enchanting thing … [i]t has memory's ear that can hear without having to hear … "

"Everywhere in India, I run into someone who is crippled from polio," he said.

Because of India's culture, the man was desperate not to be seen. By the time Bob and his interpreter reached the man, he had hidden himself behind a bush. Bob turned to his interpreter. "Make sure you translate every word I say," he said, and they walked to the crippled man. "I know exactly how you feel," Bob said and lifted his sleeve to reveal his own shriveled arm.

"The man's face went from a look of less worth than a worm into breaking into a smile," he said. Bob learned the man's only way of living was to go from house to house to beg. When the little group from the United States reached the next village, Bob visited a pastor who promised, "We will take care of him."

In the twelve years since Bob began visiting India, he has found the answer to his question. "What was once a shame for me is now a badge of honor," he said. "My arm is a tool which I use to minister to people."

Because Bob's father blessed him with words that gave him strength, Bob, empowered by his father's memory, now blesses others.

Those who influenced us may be beyond our reach to give a direct BlessBack, but we can find ways to keep their memory alive and honor them in the way we live.

You cannot do a kindness too soon,
for you never know
how soon it will be
too late.

— Ralph Waldo Emerson
Notes From a Traveler Afar

CHAPTER TEN

Regrets in Life:
Using BlessBacks to Restore

Make the most of your regrets;
never smother your sorrow,
but tend and cherish it till it comes to have a separate and integral interest.
To regret deeply is to live afresh.

— Henry David Thoreau

Isabelle Maury regrets that she had not let her grandmother know how much she loved her before she died. "Before my grandmother went to the hospital, she called me at my parents' house all the time," Isabelle wrote. "It was never a good time when she called and I was a young adult having other priorities that look so ridiculous now."

Eventually Isabelle's grandmother's health and memory deteriorated and the family had to put her in a hospital. Isabelle did not like going to visit. "I was sad and wanted to leave. This person on the bed was not the grandmother my sister and I spent vacations with in the mountains and who sang when she had a glass of wine," Isabelle said.

The week before her grandmother died, Isabelle and her sister had planned to visit her, but postponed the visit. On her last days, her grandmother was in a cold room, tensed by the pain that took her final breath. "I wished I had told her that I loved her. My parents told me that she knew as I had written to her regularly in the past and my sister and I sent her a tape recording, but to this day I still regret that I did not tell her regularly that I loved her so much, even if she drove me crazy sometimes. More than twenty years later, I still cry for my grandmother. Now I make sure that I tell my parents regularly that I love them."

When Isabelle, who lives in Seattle, turned forty, she wanted to take a family vacation, something her family had always talked about but had never done. They went to an island in French Polynesia. "My parents, who are from France, paid most of the bill for the stay for my sister and my husband and me. At seventy years old, they traveled for more than twenty-four hours. Twice they endured ten-hour flights yet greeted us with smiles at the Papeete airport where we welcomed them. They endured hot temperatures and rudimental comfort on this earthly paradise, where they loved the people as much as the beautiful island sceneries. I agree that the place is heavenly, but they did the trip for me. If that is not a proof of their love for me, I don't know what is. And my husband indulged me by making my wishes come true. His love for me was obvious."

The evening of Isabelle's birthday, she thanked her family for how much they had meant to her. "I thanked my parents for their generosity and their unconditional love, my sister for her reliable and incomparable friendship and love, and my husband for his durable love, patience and daily support for twenty years. I cried so much I had to stop reading my paper. My love for all of them was overwhelming and it took over my ability to express it to them that day. Their love is the most precious thing of my life."

We won't always be able to say our thanks to those we want to ... but we can pay our thanks forward to those who are alive.

We're only human. We won't always be on time to say our thanks to those we want to. But like Isabelle, we can pay our thanks forward to those who are alive.

Life lessons: who would we be without them? How many of us would be annoying top-down know-it-alls instead of people who allow ourselves teachable moments and are open to another's wisdom.

At our monthly Pussycat dinner two years ago, Cheryl told us about a BlessBack surprise and the feelings it generated.

Before I tell you the story, I need to tell you about Cheryl's personality. Cheryl is the living example of the French term *mise en place*. In her home, everything *is* in its place. Her closets are a marvel. Dress wear, casual wear, shoes — even colors of clothing — have their place. Even degrees of color have their place, with lime green before Christmas green and so on. Cupboards hold alphabetized cans. Life is compartmentalized. Life had to be this way, as Cheryl worked in human relations for a large company. She traveled nationwide to branch offices as often as I did to the grocery store. She could tell you her plans a year out. When the movie *Up in the Air* came to theaters, she said, "The role George Clooney played has been my job for the last eighteen months." What made her job bearable was she had empathy for everyone she laid off.

Cheryl's company went out of business in the spring of 2010. The last employee she laid off was herself. After years of living life in chronos time, Cheryl had wiggle room in the sands of kairos time. And it had come just in time.

Cheryl's parents moved from the neighborhood in which we grew up twenty years ago and now live in a southern state. Just after Cheryl lost her job, her father, Ronald, was diagnosed with non-Hodgkin lymphoma. He and Cheryl's mom came to visit Cheryl and her family.

On a late morning during their visit, Cheryl and her parents had run some errands. Cheryl talked about our friend Sue, and her mom's recent funeral. "You missed a wonderful reunion, Mom and Dad. Everybody was there from the old neighborhood."

Occasions like weddings and funerals have a way of drawing people together and Barb's funeral had made everyone who had been a part of our neighborhood realize the treasure chest we had in our little four-block square. Cheryl found herself driving toward the old Bloomington neighborhood, looking for nostalgia. She circled around the blocks, her parents making comments as they meandered.

"Look, the tree is gone from Peter's front yard."

"Remember how we could hear Jan call Cindy home for supper from two blocks away?"

"Remember how you kids used to play kick ball and elimination all night until the mosquitoes ate you alive?"

Cheryl drove up Barb and Ted's driveway. "It'll be weird to not have Barb answer," Cheryl said, fighting back tears. "I can hardly believe that Ted is now a widower."

When no one answered, they drove down their former block and saw a light on in another neighbors' house. Warren and Thelma Mead were

Cheryl's parents' best friends, and growing up, Cheryl had looked upon them as another set of grandparents. She sent them Christmas cards and when her kids were young, they often stopped by.

Sometimes life interrupts our best intentions to stay in contact with one another. Sometimes, as in Cheryl's case, we let seven years pass between visits.

Sometimes life interrupts our best intentions to stay in contact with one another.

Cheryl pulled into Warren and Thelma's driveway.

"Oh, I hate to drop in uninvited," Cheryl's mom said.

Cheryl turned to her parents. "We're here. We're going in. We can stay for five minutes, but let's just say 'hello.'"

Her parents followed her to the door.

Warren, now in his late eighties, opened the door. "Oh my gosh!" Warren said, breaking into a chuckle. "I can't believe it! Thelma! Look who is here!"

He stepped back and Cheryl saw Thelma sitting in a wheelchair in the living room. Yes, time had ticked by the years.

Warren invited them inside and they stayed for a short visit. As they talked, Cheryl looked around the room and the memories came. The walls held every painting Warren had done. She wondered if she went downstairs if she would still find in the basement rec room a wall mural of a log, frog, bear and moose he had painted from an old Hamm's beer commercial. She still treasured the oil painting of a sailboat he gave her for her wedding.

They visited together for twenty minutes and seeing that Thelma was tiring, Cheryl stood. Each hugged, kissed, and said, "Let's keep in touch." Ronald opened the front door.

"Hang on a minute," Warren said. "I have something for you, Cheryl." He walked ten feet to the TV stand and pulled out a sketch pad tablet from a shelf below. He flipped through a few pages, removed a sheet and handed it to her.

It was a pencil drawing Warren had sketched of Cheryl's two daughters from a Christmas card she had sent him in 2003.

"I've been waiting for you to stop by so I could give it to you," Warren said. "I just thought you might like to have it."

"I was dumbfounded," Cheryl said to us later at dinner. "I felt everything all at once. Thrilled to see them again, shocked and surprised at Warren's beautiful gift and that he had kept it all these years. He could have mailed it. But he hadn't. He had waited to give it to me in person."

Tears flowed with her words. "And I felt guilty that I hadn't been by to see them in all these years. I was sad, too. I realized that our visit might be the last time that Warren and Thelma and my folks see each other."

"The lesson is, when you think of someone, follow through with that thought and act," she said to us. "There's an old wives' tale floating around that if you think of someone three times, you have to pick up the phone and call that person. The third time, you have to do it. It's not enough to just think about them, but you need to follow through and phone them or drive over to see them. It doesn't take much to make that effort. I wish I had been more a part of their lives these past seven years. I realize now that just because my parents moved away didn't mean I needed to give up that closeness."

Each of us has regrets. Two nights ago I passed on going to a funeral of a friend's father. I was on the other side of town visiting my son and I did not want to sit through rush hour traffic to go.

Today, I regret my decision. I missed being near this friend in her grieving hour. I missed learning about her dad, a former police officer, and hearing the stories that made up his life. I missed the memory-making of just being at the funeral with others, brought together to honor Dawn's dad.

I know that Cheryl regrets the lost time not spent with visiting Warren and Thelma, but Cheryl used her regret in a good way. She captured *what time remains*. Each time she looks at Warren's picture, she is reminded again of what life is about: Relationships.

Daily BlessBacks

At a breakout session at a conference, I learned a little about the woman seated next to me. She talked about the fleece jacket she had received from a blood donor center. "I wear this jacket," she said, "to remind me that I gave someone life-saving platelets. It reminds me in a tangible way that I did something that helped bless another to live."

My sister-in-law has an auto immune deficiency. Every three weeks her immune system is infused with gamma globulin from up to 60,000 donors. "I feel so overwhelmed when I think of all the donors' antibodies that are enabling me to live," she said. "I know I can never thank them back personally. My way to honor their gift to me is to live fully each day as best I can."

"Words, words, words...we are all capable of making others happy, or making others cry, with words," said Peggy Bissonette.

Peggy and her husband Bernard live in an assisted-living home. "It is truly a unique experience, living so closely with elderly people," Peggy said. Peggy was having trouble walking and had to use an electric-powered scooter. Her problems were corrected when three stents were put in her arteries. When she returned to the home, she walked into the dining room. "I received encouragement at every turn," Peggy said. "'Hooray for you!' 'Keep it up,' and 'How wonderful!' All marvelous, encouraging words." Peggy felt that these people, who had come together for health reasons to live, saw her now as their close friend, one whom they cared about.

"Bernard enjoys helping others by finding open seats in the dining room, pushing wheelchairs, pouring coffee, acting like an usher at our church services. He tells everyone he's just happy to be able to help. One day one of the lady residents told him, 'When I see you, I am reminded of Jesus.'

"Bernard was so completely taken aback, he was speechless," Peggy said. "We both feel we received BlessBacks and we will continue to try to look for ways to do so, too."

When You Can't Find the Person You Want to Thank

People come and go in our lives and as much as we desire and search to find that certain someone to express our thanks, we may not always succeed. To use the British phrase, he or she will remain on our "went missing" list.

In situations like this, what consoles me is to pray for the people I wish I could find to BlessBack. I may not know where my life influencers are, but God does. I ask Him to bless them, wherever they are, and for Him to bring people into their lives who will express thanks in a meaningful way.

When you cannot find the illuminator whom you want to BlessBack, you could thank another person who is similar to your life influencer.

> When you cannot find the illuminator whom you want to BlessBack, you could thank another person who is similar to your life influencer.

As a seventy-fifth birthday present to herself, JoAnn Hannaman ran an ad in the *Savage Pacer* to find some of her former students. The ad read: "JoAnn Hannaman was a teacher at Savage Elementary back in 1960 teaching first and second grade. She is requesting any former students to write her a letter with memories. She will write you back."[1]

No one answered her ad, but one student, who had her for a teacher when she taught at another school, saw the ad and sent her a birthday wish telling her he remembered that she invited the students to her home for a picnic to celebrate the end of the school year.

She was thankful for his kindness in writing, but what surprised Hannaman was the letters she received from people she didn't know. Most carried the same message: the writers had tried to find a former teacher but couldn't so they wrote to Hannaman to thank her for being a teacher instead.

CHAPTER ELEVEN

When Relationships are Estranged

But there is good news yet to hear
and fine things to be seen
Before we go to Paradise by way of Kensal Green.

— G. K. Chesterton

As a composer of sacred music, Greg Schaffner, sixty-two, found he was spending hours alone each day. He wanted people in his life but in a one-to-one situation rather than in a large-group setting. He found part-time employment with a national caregivers franchise and now, four older men receive weekly visits from Greg on an individual basis. Each one has had some sort of life-changing circumstance happen, such as a stroke, memory loss, or limited mobility. The hours of interaction between Greg and his clients has created a sweet exchange between caregiver and companion. "Being around them is a two-way street of give and get," Greg said. "I give to them, but what a gift they are to me, to see how life can be and accept the reality in that."

Greg received a caregiver's award for being a companion to these men. In his acceptance speech, he jokingly said that his life is similar to *Tuesdays with Morrie*, except in his case, his Tuesdays are spent with the son of a Kentucky moonshiner and coal miner, Wednesdays are spent with a former navy pilot who also worked in medicine, Thursdays he visits a survivor of a major stroke and Fridays, Greg visits with a widowed former farmer.

The blessings of being a caregiver to these men has had many layers of restoration for Greg. Greg had a difficult relationship with his father and years ago broke contact with him. Greg hadn't talked to him in some years when his father died. "There's a kind of normal pattern in life and one part of it is to take care of your parents as they age and die and that was not available to me," Greg said. Greg found healing and that he had purpose as a companion and caregiver to the men. "I am able to give these people, these neat men, my undivided attention, meeting them where they are and not expecting anything from them other than who they are."

Greg visits for several hours, allowing the men to tell the stories the way they want to tell them. One of Greg's clients, Roger, is upset that his brain doesn't work anymore. "He definitely has a degree of dementia and he knows it. However, he and I operate on a pretty high level. He perks up after fifteen minutes of my being there," Greg said.

Another layer of meaning for Greg is that he senses how a family should work. "You don't have to be anybody other than who you are. You are with somebody who likes being with you," he said. "These men take me in and it makes me feel so good to think that somebody would find my company so meaningful."

Visiting these men each week has also helped him with the guilt of breaking contact with his father. "Whether or not there is some resolve with my father by my doing this is a deep question," Greg said. "But in doing this work, there is a sense that you have lived your life well and that what I do now goes on the plus side of that question. This provides an opportunity to do something that I wish I had done."

Greg also sees that the natural aging process, something he had struggled with, is no longer something to be feared. "The pinnacle of career achievement is behind these men and I am allowed to see the other side of that climb," he said. "I don't know that I've reached my pinnacle yet. I hope I haven't and fear that in my own life. But there is wisdom in this older generation and it has been very healing to me. There's an acceptance of life as it is. It never occurs to me to judge these men according to what their dreams might have been or what my hopes might be for them. When I arrive it's, 'here's who they are,' and I'm glad to be around them. And doing that, it gets me away from judging myself in that way."

Sometimes, there is no common ground with people who betray and hurt us. To protect our hearts and our life, we must sever ties from the ones who damaged us. The point of this book is for you to live a resilient life, one filled with joy, and to become the healthiest, in mind, body and spirit, that you can. Under no circumstance should you put yourself in an unsafe and unhealthy situation by looking back and thinking you need to thank an unsafe person or someone who harmed you.

> *The point of this book is for you to live a resilient life, one filled with joy, and to become the healthiest, in mind, body and spirit, that you can.*

But in working with men of his father's generation, Greg found a way to resolve the irresolvable; he has received from these men an education about fear and the unknown aging process, and about living in peace. He has done so by giving a "being in the moment" BlessBack with them and let the music of human life fulfill him.

At his acceptance speech for his caregiver's award, Greg read his version of the prayer of St. Francis of Assisi. It is worth sharing as it models the BlessBack life:

> Lord,
> Make me a channel of thy care.
> Where there is loneliness, let me bring company.
> Where there is regret, let me bring hope.
> Where there is sadness, cheerfulness.
> Where there is paranoia, let me bring calm.
> Where there is confusion, let me bring clarity.
> Help me to seek to serve rather than be served.
> And to offer care to others rather than seek care from them.
> For it is in caring that we fulfill Your will for us.
> Amen.

PART THREE

How to do a BlessBack

CHAPTER TWELVE
A BlessBack Starter Kit

I expect some new phases of life this summer,
and shall try to get the honey from each moment.

— Lucy Stone

Oprah Winfrey held an extravagant party in 2005 for twenty-five women who influenced her life. *People* magazine asked her what prompted her to throw such a party. Oprah said, "I started thinking about women who had been a bridge to now in my life, and how much they mean to me."[1]

Thus far, you have been a passenger, reading other people's BlessBacks and their deliveries of them. The *Note to Self* sections prompted you to think about your past and coached you to think creatively about making your life a gratitude-filled one. Now, it is your turn to BlessBack.

BE YOU

The passenger car at the depot awaits someone. You. It's time to board and become an active vessel of gratitude, whether you use words, actions, gifts, or a combination, to express your BlessBack.

Perhaps your family of origin encouraged self-expression. Others of you may come from "be-seen-and-not-heard" roots. You may be serious; you may be carefree. Each of us has a unique personality. Some of you are extroverts and get energy from being around people. Others are introverts; too much "people time" drains your energy.

The world is a big melting pot, filled with different styles and cultures. Some people are adroit in oral spontaneity and "think on their feet." They love verbal repartee. If this is your style, use it to BlessBack. Others are crafty and may use natural fibers, textures, and colors to create one-of-a-kind gifts as an expression of thanks. Others still like actions or contributions done in honor of their life influencer. I prefer the simplicity of pen, paper, and time to develop and express my thoughts.

Whatever your background, personality or style in giving a BlessBack, be who you are and express yourself.

GATHER WHAT YOU'LL NEED

No matter what form of BlessBack you give, first you'll need to organize your thoughts. In order to be clear on why you're giving thanks, take a little trip down memory road. Gather some stationery, a notebook, some visual aids if you want, such as photographs, old ticket stubs, a souvenir or memento that relates to the person you plan to thank. Now is the time you will use your writings from the *Note to Self* sections. They were designed specifically to get you thinking about whom you want to thank, how you want to thank them and what you would say to them, given the chance. If you filled these sections out, most of your work is done.

Whatever your background, personality or style in giving a BlessBack, be who you are and express yourself.

You will simply transfer what you've written into the BlessBack method you choose. If you skipped the *Note to Self* sections, you might want to go back and write your responses to the questions, either in the book's margins or in a notebook.

The checklist on the next page is intended for the giver. It can be used as the first draft of a letter; it also can be the brainstorming that leads to the perfect event, gift, or other activity in which you choose to BlessBack your recipient.

Find a comfortable place, full of your kind of ambiance. Whether it's a velvet cushion, a window seat, a favorite chair, a den or your local coffee shop, find a calming place where you feel most at ease with yourself and surroundings. I live close to a lake and often I'll take a blanket and let the nodding sailboats and lapping waves work their magic on my creativity.

Settle into your cushion and take a sheet of paper. It's time to clear your mind by writing down what's distracting you – what you're having for dinner, bills to pay, the weather, grocery items you need, work you need to do, house repairs, etc. Put the piece of paper in your wallet or purse and as you do, remove them from your mind. Your to-do's are documented and safe. It's time to leave them behind.

> *While with an eye made quiet*
> *by the power of harmony,*
> *and the deep power of joy,*
> *We see into the life of things.*
>
> — William Wordsworth

Facing a blank page can be scary. Thoughts rush at us. What should I write, will I misspell a word, is my grammar correct, will my meaning be misconstrued? How do I say what I want to say? If you think about how you want to BlessBack your recipient, your anxiety will diminish because you will focus on the creative process. The same is true with writing a letter. If you pre-write, it will take the fear of facing a blank page away. It will also help you order what you want to say and how you want to express your thanks. A rough draft will help you get organized.

Though there is more than one way to get going, I use two methods, depending on my mood, to get my ideas down and to remind me of the points I want to make: A checklist and wheel-writing.

A BlessBack Checklist

A checklist does several things. It gives you some structure and prompts, and gets your creative juices going. You need not check off each number before you write your letter; two or three will do. When you reach the end of your checklist, your BlessBack letter will seem to write itself because you've done the pre-work to organize it.

The Checklist

1. Is there a special memory of an action your recipient did that affected you? Why did it touch you?
   Example: "I remember when we went to visit you after you moved to Seattle and you gave me a salt and pepper shaker from

your collection so I would remember our visit. I was touched that you gave me something that was important to you. I still have the little set and use it on special occasions. Every time I do, I'm reminded of you and your gesture of kindness."

2. Why do you value him and what sets him apart from others in your memory? What was unique about his attitude that made you feel loved?

    Example: "Not many people had time to listen to me in my growing-up years and something about the tone of your voice when you told me I could call you anytime made me believe you. No matter the hour I called, you always had a ready ear, and because of your nurturing, I felt secure when life around me was out of control."

3. What did you like about her? Did her larger-than-life personality and friendliness teach you confidence? Did her sense of serenity and quiet ministrations comfort you? Was someone patient and taught you a skill that is useful to you now, such as how to change oil or replace a zipper? Did they model a way of life in a way that was instructional, loving and non-threatening?

4. Did you observe her sacrifice of material or monetary gain for a more heart-satisfying life? Did she put the money toward a child's braces or education? Did she sacrifice her time or other personal resources so that another might gain?

5. What is it about his view of life — his clever puns, his willingness to be the fall guy, the donation of his time and resources — that affected you? My father's side of the family had the lamest of jokes. Sometimes, I'd hesitate to ask them anything in fear that I would yet again feed into their one-liners. "How are you feeling?" "With my fingers." "How are you?" "Fine as frog's hair." Now that my aunt is the only sibling left of six, those terrible jokes are treasures. Just as our handwriting is uniquely our own, our quirky ways reveal much of how we view life. What are your recipient's trademark sayings that you could remind her or him about, with affection?

6. Your thoughts about your life-influencer matter and so do your feelings. Give in to your feelings of how you remember the emotional "spots of time" that go with the memories.

7. Was there an event or activity you associate with them, like school plays or a golf tournament? Maybe you could always count on their help at the school you or your children attended. Did they always head up the canned goods or toy drive for the holidays?

For all of your checklist items, go back to your *Note to Self* sections — the answers may already be there.

WHEEL-WRITING

If you prefer to work in a more spontaneous, less structured way to gather your thoughts about your recipient, wheel write. Put your recipient's name in the center of a paper. (In the made-up example below, the Martins and their house is our "hub.") Create spokes out from your wheel's hub and at the top of each spoke put the memories you want to include in your letter. Once you write your specific memories (or spokes), number them in the order in which you want to use them and start to write your letter.

When I wrote my seventh grade English teacher, my spokes not only included specific ways in which she encouraged me but also included any memories I had to share of the school itself such as classrooms, hallway chaos, and clothing styles from the time period.

Let who you are shine. A BlessBack is not a competition. There is not a "best in show" ribbon for creativity, language or presentation. This is your personal, sincere way of offering a BlessBack and there is no one right way to offer one. If you prefer structure, put as much thought into your BlessBack as you like, until you feel comfortable. If you'd rather be spontaneous and creative, bask in whimsy. If you decide organizing a toy drive or starting a book club in their honor is the best BlessBack, go right ahead. Whether you decide to write a BlessBack letter and throw a party or thank your life influencer one-to-one or through the mail, your BlessBack will be meaningful because you invested your heart, time and effort into thanking your recipient.

Let who you are shine.

No matter if you use words, actions or gifts to express your BlessBack, relax and enjoy the ride as you create yours in a way that comes naturally to you. As E. M. Forster said, "Only connect."

In the depths of winter,
I finally learned that within me there lay an invincible summer.

— Albert Camus
Notes From A Traveler Afar

CHAPTER THIRTEEN
Giving a BlessBack Through Words

I get such a kick out of a particular friend of mine…
First, she scours for THE perfect card,
so appropriate in fact, only I would "get" it.
It's sort of a lost art. Sending cards, I mean.
The entire envelope looks like a present.
The return address labels have a story all their own.
She uses Walt Disney World tape across the back
and has the cutest cartoon stamps.
She writes with squiggles and swirls and stars
which shows her playful, fun personality.
God, I love my friend. Thanks for her.

— A poem found on a Facebook wall

A couple of days ago, a man ahead of me in line at the checkout counter wrote a check and as he did, I noticed he made his '8' differently than I do.

The way we write our numbers and our words, whether in cursive or print, is our esprit de corps. Some of us write in cursive, some print, while others use a combination. Our writing style is as unique and personal as it gets.

The same holds true for what we put in our sentences. Madeleine L'Engle said that "creative involvement" occurs between an author and a reader. When we write or receive a letter, an exchange happens. We are "imagining … visualizing … seeing facial expressions, hearing the inflection of voices," L'Engle wrote. The letter writer and the reader, like the author and reader, "'know' each other; they meet on the bridge of words."[1]

A Concrete Bridge to Being Thanked

Your BlessBack letter will bring encouragement to your recipient, and if kept, will add continued meaning to his or her life. On a down day, your recipient can open it, be re-blessed, and in so doing, chase the shadows of loneliness or insignificance away. Your written thanks authenticates your life influencer's goodness.

Helps Clarify the Memory of Being Thanked

Sometimes when verbally thanked or shown gratitude, people get embarrassed and flustered; they brush away the compliment, don't believe it, or miss the positive words said about them. A letter is a permanent record of your feelings, and because it is, it is significant. With your BlessBack letter, your recipient holds tangible evidence that says, "So-and-so said this to me. She said my words and actions changed her life in these specific ways."

Gretchen's mother, Rollie Brandt, is an artist. Her specialty is realistic paintings of barns, things found in nature and "kids being kids." Her work is included in calendars and greeting cards, and has graced more than thirty publication covers. When Gretchen's wedding day to Wayde approached, Gretchen designed a BlessBack to her parents in a way they would appreciate — through drawings

Your written thanks authenticates your life influencer's goodness.

and childhood memories. On the night of her wedding, Gretchen left two spiral-bound books, one for Mom, one for Dad, on their pillows.

After the wedding, as the bride's parents got ready for bed, they spied the booklets. Here is an example of what they opened:

I remember when I broke the mug I made you, when I dropped it while wrapping it. You had to put together your own gift!

I remember when you slept overnight in the igloo you built.

Image courtesy of Gretchen Fleener

CHRISTMAS MEMORIES

I remember the good eggs you make on Christmas morning.

I remember going to get our Christmas tree and sawing it down.

I remember you reading us the "St. Nick" story from the Childcraft book.

I remember going to the "big mall," Burnsville Center, with you + Heidi, to Christmas shop for Mom.

I remember when you made us skating rinks. That was so cool!

Gretchen's drawings and words filled the book's pages.

To her mom:

> *"I remember when you used to pin notes to my shirt for the teacher."*
>
> *"I remember the 'lunch ticket box' you made out of a Band-Aid container."*

To her dad:

> *"I remember sitting on your lap on your chair, reading my new 'letter books' for kindergarten."*
>
> *"I remember going on 'dates' with you! That was fun!"*
>
> *"I remember when you took care of me when I was sick and stayed home from school."*

Gretchen did two things when she gave her parents the books. She thought about how it would feel for her parents to give their daughter over to a new life. She also thought about the past and, using her memories, created the books as a way to express thanks for what her parents had done for her; moreover she showed them that the way they lived their lives had not gone unnoticed.

"It took me three days to read them without tears," Rollie said. "This is the best gift Gretchen ever gave us. We love them!"

LEAVES A LEGACY

When Jo Ellen Coleman's father died, another family took her under their wing. They treated her as if she were their daughter. When Jo Ellen learned a party was being thrown for her "surrogate" father in the summer of 2006, she wrote the patriarch and wife a BlessBack letter, thanking them for their kindnesses to her when she was a young girl.

At the birthday party, Jo Ellen saw her letter, framed and hung on a prominent wall in the family's home.

With a letter, you leave a legacy, not only for your life influencer to remember, but also for your life influencer's family. A future relative may read your letter, learn the kind of person his uncle or grandparent was, and gain a feeling of pride.

Appreciation can make a day, even change a life.

Your willingness to put it into words is all that is necessary.

— Margaret Cousins

THE MEANING OF LIFE: GRATEFULNESS

My seventh grade English teacher, Mrs. Fatchett, has held a warm place in my heart for more than forty-one years and for a great many of them I wanted to thank her for being a life influencer. On the last day of school in June 1971, I watched other students toss their three-ring notebooks in the garbage as they left class.

I too, extended my three-ring notebook, a brown binder Dad had given to me from his work, over the wastebasket. On the cover were two glow-in-the-dark orange sticky plastic handprints that said, "Keep off," "Julie," and a giant "Love" crafted in decorative letters in blue ballpoint. Oblivious to the last day of school noise around me, I opened the binder and saw the royal blue wide-lined spiral notebook with the words "My Journal" on its cover. Inside were months' worth of daily entries with Mrs. Fatchett's check marks of approval on the pages. Entries included my bowling averages, favorite teachers, weekly comments on my loathed half-hours of practicing piano complaints, ongoing friendships and boy dramas. A February entry had a heart-shaped "Happy Valentine's Day, Mrs. Fatchett!"

Behind the diary were my writing assignments: A poem, some short stories, and my first attempt at a novel called *The Thief*, whose heroine was a young female sleuth in Keds and pedal pushers.

I closed the binder and tucked it to my chest. I would use the binder as my beacon of courage to do what I thought I wanted: To write stories.

That beacon resides in my barrister bookcase next to my portfolio binder of published articles. For a great many years — whenever I doubted my writing abilities — I opened that binder, re-read Mrs. Fatchett's simple yet encouraging comments, and let her words propel me to restart an article when I was stumped.

In the fall of 2004 I was given the opportunity to finish college after two failed attempts. I looked at that binder and knew I was ready to fell my dragons — especially the science and math ones.

I started with one class, to get "my brave on," and soon was taking four classes a semester. Most days I came home exhausted from learning about new neuron passages and Pythagorean's theorem. My family was patient and understood my deep desire to obtain a diploma, and many nights they ignored my simple menus and the undone laundry.

I finished my sophomore year in December 2006 and began to breathe a little easier, having finally learned how to study. I was excited to start my junior year. My mind drifted to Mrs. Fatchett. *Someday,* I thought, *I need to thank her.*

My first day of class the following February, I dialed the school district's phone number where I thought she'd last worked. The district said she had retired in 2001 but they likely still sent her her pension check. I dialed the pensions department, explained that I needed to find a former teacher. The woman who answered said that due to confidentiality reasons she could not tell me Mrs. Fatchett's phone number. I told her I was on a mission to thank a teacher for what she had meant in my life. The woman said, "Hold on a second."

I waited for a minute or two on the line. She came back on. "I just spoke with Mrs. Fatchett. She said to tell you that she would love to talk to you. Here's her phone number."

I took a deep breath and dialed, only to hear her voice on her answering machine. I left a message and finished my drive.

Mrs. Fatchett called me back when I was in the middle of the student lounge surrounded by twenty-year-old students studying. I tried not to blush, knowing the entire area was hearing me thank Mrs. Fatchett for what she had meant to me.

Mrs. Fatchett was sweet and seemed happy I had called. I told her I had something for her so we arranged to meet for dinner.

I wrote a letter to her, photocopied my journal, my stories, and poems, and had them bound.

This is a portion of what I wrote:

February 20, 2007

Dear Mrs. Fatchett:

Thank you so much for being willing to meet with me after all these years. To get the chance to visit with you again means the world to me.

I realize you've probably not given me a thought for thirty-six years nor do you remember me. You, however, have stayed with me, tucked near and dear to my heart since September of 1971.

Yes, we really do have to go back that far, to when Nixon was president, Twiggy and I wore go-go boots and you had a modified bouffant hairdo. The last time we had a conversation, America was at war with the North Vietnamese, my dad drove a Nash rambler and you wore a dress every day to teach us seventh grade English.

And me? My imagination was in full swing when I read Nancy Drew and Mary Stewart's Nine Coaches Waiting. *When I ironed dishtowels and pillowcases, it left me plenty of time to plot a story. By the time I got to junior high, I was ready to write something.*

That's where you come in, Mrs. Fatchett. Somehow, some way, you saw some kind of writing potential and coaxed it out of me. You did this in a silly, marvelous way. You made English class the funnest place to be. English class was whimsical. It was magic, and with you teaching us, it was entertaining.

I don't remember a thing that we read. What I remember were the "10s" on my papers, the freedom to express what I needed to through writing. I learned that writing could be whatever I wanted it to be.

We had to write daily in our journals. (Something I try to stick to even now.) It wasn't so much what we wrote, it was the act of writing that you taught us. Writing a journal entry forced me daily to write words on a page. That journal was my first public writing. It was for an audience – you. How that audience mattered to me, for you believed in me. ...

... I floundered at my first attempt at college, failing English Composition twice before I dropped out. I didn't take an English class until I was in my early thirties. Much to my delight I landed a great teacher who knew, as you did, the power of journaling and the freedom in writing it produces ...

... None of my published writing accomplishments would have happened if it wasn't for you – your encouraging hand, comments and happy face. Many times I came into other teachers' classrooms and they hardly looked at students. You interacted with us, you cracked jokes.

You had a delightful sense of humor, yet at the same time taught us and taught us well.

It's because of you that I had the courage to dream big. Thank you for the memories and thank you for being a great teacher with a big personality.

Blessings, Julie

As I entered the restaurant where we had arranged to meet, I saw that Mrs. Fatchett was already seated, waiting. She looked the same to me except for wisps of grey hair and a missing bouffant hairstyle. Her big eyes were just as expressive. Her personality still as zany and effervescent as I remembered.

As we ate, sharing memories of my junior high years, I read her my letter. I gave her a bound set of some published articles and my 1971 diary and the stories from her class. As she paged through the spiral-bound book, sometimes she laughed, sometimes she told a story about a former teacher or the principal we had. I pulled out my yearbook, where she had written kind words to me.

She looked at my yearbook picture and kindly said, "I do remember you. I remember you sat on the right side of the room, towards the back."

The night took us into another world, where no consciousness of hours existed.

Toward the evening's end, her laughter faded and she grew serious. "You know, for years I saved all my attendance books, hoping former students would call me and tell me about their lives so I would be able to go to my little books, see their grades, and remember where they sat in my classroom. But no one did so I threw them when I retired."

I am glad I paused in 1971 at the garbage can. Forty years later, that binder inspired me to give Mrs. Fatchett tangible proof that she had changed a life and affected someone in a way she could never have foreseen.

A week later, a little note came in my mail:

Tues. Feb. 27, 2007

Dearest Julie:

It isn't often that a teacher receives validation of her work or even gets to see students after they leave her classroom. Last week was extraordinary and having the chance to see you and talk with you was the icing on the cake.

There's no way to thank you enough for the trip down memory lane plus the great dinner. Do you know that I sat and read your journal and your articles before I went to sleep that night? ...

Thank you again. You made thirty-five years of hard work and dedication all worthwhile.

Love always, Pat Fatchett

Never underestimate the power of your words. Whether written or spoken, they will make a difference because you spoke to a person's heart.

Never underestimate the power of your words.

REMEMBERING SOMEONE'S LOVE

In the course of writing this book, people wanted to know if they couldn't just say their thanks, rather than write a letter. Of course you can.

On a particularly hard day in the midst of a divorce, LuAnn Seymour decided to give a BlessBack to her aunt.

LuAnn's father died when she was five and her mother when she was seven. Jane Cummings, her mother's sister, agreed to raise LuAnn and her brother, but it wasn't long before the siblings transferred their grief into resentment toward their aunt. "We had just lost our parents," LuAnn said. "I blamed my aunt for a lot of my unhappiness."

At the time, LuAnn didn't understand that her aunt had lost something too. "I was just a kid," LuAnn said. "I didn't realize that my aunt had not only lost her sister, but she had also lost her freedom. I didn't understand that she would have been an empty-nester in three months once her youngest daughter married. You never think about what somebody gives up for you," LuAnn said.

On a February day she called her aunt. "I felt moved to thank her because of the struggles I was going through," LuAnn said. "I was separating from my husband of twenty-five years. I just kept thinking about how difficult it must have been to raise us. I had worked through some troubled times with addictions with my aunt's help. Even though many times I've felt thankful, I had never said so to her."

"I needed her support and once again, she was there," LuAnn said. "She gave me the encouragement I needed." As the conversation deepened, LuAnn thanked her aunt for raising her, telling her she knew she had been difficult to raise.

Shocked by her niece's kind and unexpected words, her aunt thanked LuAnn using words of appreciation that LuAnn badly needed to hear that day. "I love you," her aunt said. "And LuAnn — you were easy to love."

LuAnn's advice to others is, "If you have a lot of gratitude, you need to let the person know how much she means to you. I had wanted to thank her for so long. It took forty-seven years for her to hear it, but she heard it.

"For me, the feeling that came from thanking her ... I was just incredibly emotional. When you do really feel grateful, there's a lot of emotion behind the words 'thank you.' It was a release for me."

When you're giving a verbal BlessBack, you're expressing your love and thanks to that person. Your recipient comes away from the memory saying, "This person does care about me. I am important to her."

Thirty-nine-year-old Kelly Johnson is a stay-at-home mom with two young daughters. As a child psychologist, Kelly knows the peer pressures her daughters will face in their teen years and works hard to instill in them a healthy self-esteem now. She also knows the important role their father Michael has in their development.

Michael travels a lot in his job working with schools to build safe and mentally healthy environments. Still, there are days when his schedule takes him away for five days at a time and Kelly is the only visible parent.

One spring, Kelly's husband's schedule included being home for the whole week and Kelly took a break from parenting to attend an event sponsored by her church.

A young woman who had learned that Kelly was married to Michael talked to her during a break. "Before you and Michael met," Emily said, "Michael was my summer camp counselor when I was a teenager. He was so nice to me. I was feeling self-conscious about how I looked in a swimsuit at the beach one day and your husband happened to hear me say so. I'll never forget his response. He told me, 'Don't you ever say that about yourself again. You are beautiful just the way you are. Now get in that water and have some fun.' His words have stayed with me all these years. He really helped me develop a healthy esteem about myself."

Kelly started to cry. "You have no idea how much what you just told me means to me, to learn that the man I married genuinely feels this way about people." She told Emily that she had been worried about her girls growing up. "By your telling me this I know Michael will love my daughters just the way he did you and instill self-worth in them when they are teenagers, too."

In *Sound Business,* Julian Treasure states that sound, with the exception of nature, is human-made and that the most powerful sound is the human voice. "It's the only sound that can start or stop a war … create amazing technologies … bring people together … and of course say, 'I love you.'"[2]

Your recipient will love and appreciate any form of giving thanks. Ralph Freeman, who sang at the 2010 National Prayer Breakfast, said in a recent interview that the ears are the doorway to a person's heart. "If someone talks to you and gives you poetry through the ears, if they say something that brings memories to you through the ears, if they sing a song to you through the ears, it touches your heart like nothing else can," Ralph said. "And when you take words and set them to music, it's like having a therapy session."[3]

The human voice...is the only sound that can start or stop a war... and of course say, 'I love you.'[2]

Listening to others edifies our souls. It's just as Freeman said. The human voice is the most powerful noise.

Some Options to Present your BlessBack

Where you choose to give your BlessBack is up to you. So is how you present it. You may want to read your letter aloud, maybe even from memory. Nerves are always present. Practice reading your letter aloud in front of the mirror. Just repeating it will make you get used to the sound of your voice and its inflections.

If you do choose to memorize your letter, don't memorize the lines verbatim. You will sound like a robot when you say it.

Instead, take an index card and write down in bullet form the reasons you've stated that you are thankful to your recipient in your letter. Don't write complete sentences. Just phrases will do. Another option is to just write down your reasons using key words. No, you won't have said everything exactly as the letter says, but you will sound natural and sincere in your delivery. Give the person the letter to take home and read privately later.

Perhaps my Mrs. Fatchett BlessBack story has triggered your memory and you've got someone, like Mister Rogers said in one of his children's programs, "...someone in your life that just the very thought of makes you feel better." Perhaps you can't wait to reach out to her.

If you're like me, perhaps just thinking about paying a BlessBack visit to someone gives you a stomach ache. The fear monster rouses up a host of doubts in the "I" and "They" categories. "I'll go blank and forget what I want to say." "I won't say what I want to say." "I'll do it next month when I'm less busy." "They might reject me." "They won't recognize me." "They won't get it." "They won't care."

I understand what fear can do. I put off finishing my college degree for more than thirty years because I feared that I lacked the ability to pass certain subjects. I was embarrassed when I thought of how old I would be when I received my degree until my friend, Jane Kise, who has authored twenty books in that same time frame, said to me, "Won't you be the same age in four years, anyway?"

When I finally received my degree, the self-shaming muses went away. The "I wish I would have's" have turned into "I'm so glad I did." Fear only cripples our actions whereas each day we pursue our achievements, it takes us farther down the road.

To ease your fears about doing a BlessBack, devote a small amount of time to preplan it. Use the checklist and consciously develop what you want to say. You'll gain confidence that your words are valid and express what you wanted to say. This may not conquer all your nerves, but it will diminish them.

To ease your fears about doing a BlessBack, devote a small amount of time to preplan it.

Let Elisabeth Elliot's story help you, too.

Elisabeth Elliot, along with her husband, Jim, were missionaries to Ecuador. Members of a primitive tribe killed Elisabeth's husband. Despite the loss, Elizabeth wanted to continue her mission work, but she was afraid for herself and her children. Elizabeth's decision was made, however, when a friend said, "Do it afraid."[4]

The idea is to write it
so that people hear it
and it slides through the brain
and goes straight to the heart.

— Maya Angelou
Notes From a Traveler Afar

CHAPTER FOURTEEN

Do a BlessBack Act

*How wonderful it is that nobody need wait a single moment
before starting to improve the world.
You can be the change you want to see in the world.*

— Anne Frank

Mel is a retired pastor who loves to fish, but in his eighties, he no longer has a boat or the strength to handle one. Greg Harms has known and loved Pastor Mel since he pastored Greg's church growing up. "At summer camp, Mel would ask if I wanted to go fishing," Greg said, "and I always said, 'Yes!'"

Mel would say, "Go get your fishing gear and let's go."

Greg, a dentist in his fifties, still sees Mel as a patient twice a year. "And every time he asks me if I've been fishing," Greg said. "One day, I got to remembering how he always took us fishing and I appreciated that he thought of us and took us. So I asked him if he wanted to go to my cabin for a weekend and do some fishing. He said, 'I would love to go fishing again. I haven't been fishing in several years.'"

The men arrived at Greg's cabin on Moose Lake near Grand Rapids, Minnesota and fished the evening for walleye. The next afternoon, Greg asked Mel if he wanted to give Muskie-fishing a try.

"Yeah. Let's go!" Mel said.

As Greg trolled along the weed lines, Mel cast his lure and let it drift behind the boat. The men spotted a loon with two babies and Mel wanted a picture of them and handed Greg his camera. Just as Greg trolled over toward the loons, a Muskie struck Mel's line. He handed

Greg his rod.

"Nope," Greg said. "This one's all yours."

After several times of the fish making a run from the boat, finally Mel was able to reel it in. Greg scooped it with a net and measured the fish. It was a forty-inch Muskie.

"I can't believe it," Mel said, as Greg snapped pictures of Mel holding the fish before they released it.

"I think it was probably the last good fight with a fish Mel will have," Greg said. "But I just wanted to provide the opportunity for Mel to maybe catch a big one as my way of saying thanks to him for his godly influence."

Both men will never forget what they experienced that weekend.

A BlessBack action is just what you might think it is. BlessBack acts are a hands-on approach to thanking someone in your life. It can be experienced in a moment with your recipient, or it can be an action given that expresses your thanks about your recipient. It is demonstrational in that you act out your BlessBack in a unique way. There are those of us who feel more comfortable when we can help another by doing something, whether it is taking someone fishing like Greg did with Mel, or helping someone move, or repairing someone's deck, rather than expressing it by way of a letter.

BlessBack acts are a hands-on approach to thanking someone in your life.

BlessBack acts have many benefits. They can:

EASE YOUR RECIPIENT'S LIFE

In my town, a young woman's husband died from a fast-growing cancer. The widow, Lisa, was overwhelmed with all the things normally taken care of by Jeff, her husband. Shortly after Jeff died, her garage's foundation sank and she could no longer park in her garage. Three men, neighbors who had been friends of Jeff's, suddenly showed up on a Sunday afternoon with special equipment, raised the garage floor, and fixed the off-kilter garage door tracks. When she asked them what they were doing, one of them said, "We're guys. This is the only way we could figure out how to express to you how much Jeff's friendship meant to us."

While a written note might make Lisa feel better, from a practical standpoint, fixing the garage floor made her life better. Each time she opens the garage door, she remembers their BlessBack.

CREATE A BETTER LIFE

The June day in 1967 was hot and humid in Mount Airy, a quaint section of Philadelphia. Sheri Boyer, fifteen, and her sister and mother had arrived two days before from Minnesota. Sheri was accustomed to the heat and humidity, but the essence of Pennsylvania's history was foreign to her. In this state, the Union's second born, ancient brick roads still whispered patriot songs.

This was her first of many trips back east. She was staying with her uncle Gene Boyer and his family in an old judge's mansion on Chestnut Street.

As Sheri drank from the kitchen faucet, she glanced out the window. Her uncle was rubbing down the 1962 Studebaker she and her mom had driven here. Sheri smiled. Her uncle was always looking for ways to help others.

She went to join him in the driveway. "What you are doing?" she said.

"I'm just trying to see if I can remove some of this rust from your mom's car," he said. "It's pretty bad."

"But how can you do that?" she asked. "It's rusted right through the steel." Though the coupe was still worthy of a glance or two, it had experienced deep wounds to its once-stylish physique.

He explained the steps involved in restoring the car. Sheri was thrilled that he wanted to make the car look good. It was her best chance of having a cool car, an important virtue at fifteen. After all, the "Studee" did boast black alligator bucket seats.

Uncle Gene seemed to understand *cool*. He also understood Sheri at a time when she was becoming disillusioned about life. He sensed a divorce coming between Sheri's parents. Keen to the needs of others, he valued her inquisitive nature and understood her need for attention and answers to questions about life and family.

To pay for their trip while in Mount Airy, Sheri's mother did secretarial work for the European Evangelistic Crusade. Sheri's seven-year-old sister, Becky, played with the next-door neighbor's children. Sheri kept busy playing on an old upright piano in the mansion's living room.

There was no doubt she loved to play but lacked confidence due to family — renowned, masterful musicians, one of whom had once made a living performing with the Rat Pack — who had exacting standards for Sheri.

But here, inside Uncle Gene's house, Sheri found the encouragement she needed from him. She taught herself improvisation inside his home-away-from-home and gained healing and confidence each day. With each note she played, freedom came. "I have always believed that those summer days were the renaissance of my life," she said.

His influence didn't stop with Sheri. Within his extended family, Uncle Gene initiated counseling and conversation that prompted a healing process. "Uncle Gene questioned the family dynamics with its ideological theologies and religiosities and challenged us to talk to each other in new ways that affirmed and were less critical," Sheri said.

As one of the first Protestant missionaries to France after the second war, Gene started his ministry at twenty-two, standing on Parisian street corners in the mid-1950s. He also served as a NATO chaplain and traveled throughout Europe and North Africa planting churches and preparing seminary students for outreach. To many, he became known as the Billy Graham of France. "Uncle Gene is a historian, a champion for the underdog and he is my hero," Sheri said. "Because of his example in my life, I held steadfast to my faith despite extraordinary, painful circumstances. To him, I will be forever grateful." Those "circumstances" include her parents divorcing and losing her only siblings, one as an infant, and Becky in a drowning accident.

While Sheri could never repay her uncle for his impact on her life, an opportunity came in 1999 for her to give him a BlessBack. In collaboration with various European dignitaries, *Mission to the World,* the organization with whom Gene was affiliated, hosted a fifty-year celebration to honor his ministry and many contributions to France. Her other uncle, Jerè, who had led the music ministry of the missionary team for thirty-five years, was also included in the celebration.

Sheri had always wanted to travel to France and made plans to join in the honoring of her uncles. She prepared a surprise for the celebration. Though her mother had died the previous year, Sheri saved her mother's boxes of mementos, old pictures, sermon notes, crusade posters, and other items from Gene and Jerè's ministry, and she made a scrapbook.

Arriving in the southern river town of Anduze, she was escorted to her lodgings — de Cazenove family castle, set on the highest hill overlooking the town.

The ceremony was held in a centuries-old Roman temple. Gene's trumpet fanfare reverberating around the stone walls only added to the celebration. Afterward Sheri gave her uncle the scrapbook. "Thank you so much for coming, Sheri, and thank you for this beautiful gift of memories you made. I will treasure it always," he said.

Sheri's trip to France was her BlessBack to Uncle Gene, but her uncle made sure she didn't leave without one of her own. Knowing her love of history and ancestry, Gene took her to *Le Museé du Désert,* where Sheri saw how Huguenots hid from their oppressors. She also visited remnants of slave ships which bespoke of her ancestors who were persecuted for their faith.

Lastly, her uncle gave her a Huguenot cross. Traditionally adorned with either a dove or a tear, Huguenot crosses first appeared in use during the wars of 1562-98. "I wear this cross as a symbol of my heritage, and my own personal journey of faith and freedom," Sheri said. "And for what Uncle Gene will always mean to me."

RENEW SOMEONE'S SPIRIT

Alicia Tesch, recently forced from her home because of a life-changing tragedy, couldn't believe it when forty friends moved the contents of her home from one house to another in twenty-four hours. "To receive something like this ... all you can do is accept it and be forever moved by what they did," she said. "Every time I walk into my new home I remember and appreciate how much love I was shown during the worst time of my life."

JOIN IN THE BATTLE FOR A BETTER LIFE

I took my sister-in-law to one of her chemo treatments and entered the room where cancer patients were receiving treatments. As I sat with Diane for hours, I realized they were not cancer patients. They were cancer fighters.

When you BlessBack act, your presence shows another that you are walking alongside her as she lives and sometimes fights for life.

When you BlessBack act, your presence shows another that you are walking alongside her as she lives and sometimes fights for life. You are as close to the battlefield as you can get.

Your act of gratitude may be something done once, or become a cherished habit. For example, a friend reads psalms to a retired pastor with macular degeneration every week, bringing him comfort, renewing his faith, and ministering to both their spirits. Another reads her mother's favorite poems to her every Friday — her eyes are bad. They take turns memorizing the stanzas. The daughter offers this as her BlessBack and because her mother is a former English professor, it's also a way for these two women to share something they both love.

But your BlessBack does not have to linger in someone's life to make the act meaningful. Sometimes, the stillness in a moment is the thanks back to your recipient. And it is enough. It is *satise*, in the giving and receiving of a BlessBack.

> *You gave me your time, the most thoughtful gift of all.*
>
> — Dan Zadra

HELP PEOPLE ACHIEVE THEIR DREAMS

Forty years had passed since Barb Guertin was a junior high cheerleader, but she took a risk and wrote her childhood friend a BlessBack letter.

To my old friend,

Many years ago there was a certain person who was so kind to me, for whom I am forever grateful, and that was you, Tiffany.

You may not even remember me, but I was a young girl in a family of eight kids. We had a big farm out in the country. My dad worked two jobs to support our family. There was never any extra money for school activities, but cheerleading was free to join. We had to practice every night after school. At the end of several weeks, we had try-outs to see which girls would be chosen for cheerleading.

Tiffany, you were so kind to me. You were one year older and had already made cheerleading the year before. You asked me to come over to your home and do my cheering jumps in front of your large patio window. Now, this was some home. It was a beautiful home and your dad was a doctor. I was so happy that you helped me with my cheers and with getting my split jumps just perfect.

I was the seventh child of eight and I didn't feel I received much attention. It felt wonderful that I got attention from you. Well, the school judges only picked ONE seventh grade girl to be a cheerleader. The other girls were in eighth and ninth grade. To my surprise, they picked me. That was because of the expert help from you, my friend. I was only thirteen. I blossomed from this experience in my life. I was now one of the popular girls in seventh grade (or I felt I was). It helped me have much more confidence in the following teen years.

This letter is to tell you how grateful I am for the help you gave me so many years ago. It really had a huge impact on my life that you cared enough to help a small little country girl become important and special in my school.

You are a very special person to me. I wanted you to know how you changed my life when I was so young. I felt so grateful that you were there.

Barb Guertin

"Tiffany wrote me a nice note, saying that she did not know that she had touched my life and she thanked me for writing," Barb said. "Tiffany said, 'You never know how you touch a person. I'm glad I helped you out.' After forty years, she hadn't remembered helping me."

But, Tiffany Johnson made all the difference in the world helping Barb achieve her dreams.

At nineteen, Kathryn McCarthy found herself pregnant and laid off from her job. She moved in with her father and readied herself to give up her baby. "I was struggling," she said. "I didn't know if I had the heart to be a mom. I'm not a baby magnet. I don't think all babies are cute." The best gift for her baby, Kathryn felt, was to give him to a family who could provide a loving and caring environment. She contacted an adoption agency and they found a set of adoptive parents.

A week before her son was born in May 1985, Kathryn went to bed and during the night was awakened by God. "God told me He would take care of me if I was obedient," Kathryn said. "I woke up with a 'knowing' I didn't have before. I woke up with a mother's heart and knew what to do."

She informed her parents of her decision and told the adoption agency that she was not giving up her child. "I didn't have a stick of furniture. I didn't have a name for the baby. I didn't have a job. And I had to convince the baby's father, too, that we keep the baby," she said.

The father agreed to help raise their son and their Irish redheaded boy entered the world. Kathryn named him James, came home, and found a job as an apartment property manager, which gave her a place for her and her son to live. Eventually, she fell in love with Lee Reeves, who had two children. They married, had another child together, and raised their blended family of four children.

Today, twenty years later, Kathryn and Lee's house has two private apartments for young single moms who work and attend college full-time. Because Kathryn keeps rent affordable, she enables the young women to work toward their own dreams. "God gave me a promise, and I have always wanted to help other young single moms." Providing the women safe and supportive housing, Kathryn said, is her way of offering a BlessBack to God.

The beauty of Kathryn's BlessBack act is that it is active and practical, helping people here on earth. "Being a single mom is almost impossible unless somebody reaches out. Especially in a Christian society, single moms feel 'less than.' You've got to step in. There needs to be grace. If somebody would have done for me what I'm doing for them, I would have had the courage to go to school. I would have been bolstered if someone would have sacrificed for me."

> *Remember, we are all affecting the world every moment,*
> *whether we mean to or not.*
> *Our actions and states of mind matter,*
> *because we are so deeply interconnected with one another.*

— Ram Dass

BlessBack actions can be big or small, done with a moment's thought or used to build a lifetime around. Below are more ideas for BlessBack actions; may they spur your own.

BlessBack actions can be big or small, done with a moment's thought or used to build a lifetime around.

Send Cookies to Someone in the Military

Carol Schilling's daughter, Dori, lived in the United States while engaged to Andrew Tierney, a British Royal Air Force officer. Back in the states, Carol, known by her children's friends as the ultimate cookie baker, made it a point to send care packages to Andrew every month while he was in Afghanistan.

Carol included in those packages bug spray, new socks, towelettes and cookies. Carol packaged the cookies — her renowned chocolate chip, oatmeal, and monster cookies — in small packages so Andrew could pass them to his fellow soldiers and commanding officer. Some cookies arrived broken, but it didn't matter to the soldiers. They had survived on Ready-to-Eat meals for months and the homemade treats tasted delicious.

Grateful that Carol had taken the time to think of him and those under his command, Andrew made all his soldiers send Carol thank-you notes. Most said, "Thanks so much for the cookies. They tasted unbelievably great."

One note in particular, though, made Carol chuckle. "Thank you so much for the cookies," the note stated. "And should you be in need of a husband, you know where to find me." It was signed by Andrew's commanding officer.

Jim and Mary Beth Roane's winter home was in Naples, Florida. While there, Mary Beth found their eleven-month-old son, Jack, floating face down in the pool. Jim rescued him and Mary Beth began CPR and got Jack's pulse going. Paramedics rushed Jack to the hospital. The Roanes stayed at the local Ronald McDonald House (RMH). Their family, which included their three other children from three- to eight-years-old, was housed, fed, and counseled.

Sadly, after five days, Jack died. Shortly after Jack's death, Jim and Mary Beth joined RMH's board because of the love and nurturing received from the organization during the family's darkest hours. Jim took time off from work and involved himself in fundraising activities for the Minnesota chapter, serving as board president. Mary Beth still volunteers as a grief counselor to those who also lost a child.

"In a way, working with the RMH helps us to keep Jack's memory alive. It makes his short life meaningful," Mary Beth said.

In October 2010, the Roanes helped establish the fifth RMH. The "House" at Minneapolis Children's Hospital is the largest RMH inside of a hospital of its kind in the world. With 8,500 square feet, the complex has sixteen guest rooms. It serves dinner on average to seventy people each night, helping four hundred families each month. "We wish no family ever had to walk down this journey, but for those of us who are on that journey, it's important to note that there is a group of people who care about your situation and are willing to facilitate a best-case scenario for you while you are in your darkest hour," Mary Beth said. "Through this service, we are able to lighten the load for many families facing a medical crisis with their child."

GIVE A "LIVING EULOGY"

As a successful real estate developer, one of Bruce Peterson's greatest pleasures was mentoring young businessmen. Ten years after he began mentoring, he was invited to dinner by one of them. When he arrived at the restaurant, all eight men he mentored sat at the table. During the meal, each man shared how Bruce had made a difference in his life. "It was a significant night," Bruce recalls. "I was made aware that I had helped people over the years and that the years I had spent mentoring had been worth it."

SMALL CHANGE CAN EQUAL BIG CHANGE

Becky Tracey wanted to say thank-you to missionaries she knew, some of whom had financial needs, special projects, or health problems. She collected the spare change she saved each month and asked a fellow employee, Jennifer, to join her. "I still have only one person matching my donation, but even just one means the change goes twice as far," Becky said. The two women called their program "The Change Brigade" and within months they had accumulated $344.84 to give to missionaries. "I'm always surprised at how fast the change adds up when you make it intentional," Becky said, who still sets her small change aside for charity.

GIVE A LOT

Al's Breakfast is a narrow restaurant in Dinkytown near the University of Minnesota's Minneapolis campus. Just ten feet wide, it only has counter seating. Al Bergstrom, who owned the restaurant before he passed away, served breakfasts, mostly to poor college students who sometimes couldn't pay for their meal. Al was heard to say on more than one occasion, "That's okay. You'll pay me when you can."

And the students did. Returning as professionals, some paid $1,000 at the cash register for their breakfast saying, "This is what I figure I owe you — with interest."

That narrow little restaurant provided students a gateway to a thankful life through Al's generosity. Al received BlessBacks because he had cared more about nourishing them than about being paid.

DO A BLESSBACK VISIT ON YOUR VACATION

For times when the person you want to thank lives out of town, consider taking a vacation and bringing your BlessBack with you.

September in New England is beautiful, but Rick and I had more in mind than just celebrating our thirtieth wedding anniversary when we visited the East Coast in 2010.

For years I had wanted to BlessBack Sandy and Dick Reed who live in New Hampshire. I wanted to thank Sandy for her giving me confidence as a teenager when I babysat their children, Jeff, Heather and Jennifer. Sandy gave me free rein in her house. I baked, cooked, and because I felt so comfortable in her home, I cleaned and rearranged her utility closet on a regular basis. Looking back on that memory makes me cringe in embarrassment. I wasn't snooping. I honestly wanted to organize her closet. Now I am red-faced. Yet she never made comment. Her words were ones of praise and encouragement.

For times when the person you want to thank lives out of town, consider taking a vacation and bringing your BlessBack with you.

A short search on the Internet gave me the Reeds' phone number. I called and told them we were coming that way in the fall. They seemed genuinely happy to hear from me. I told them that we would love to meet them for lunch.

Rick and I met them at their home in Rye Beach. The afternoon was a non-stop catch-up on each other's lives. It had been twenty-five years.

We went for lunch right where the Piscataqua River separates New Hampshire from Maine. I ate my first lobster roll overlooking boats trolling under the bridge against the backdrop of a centuries-old brick-steepled-church and board-and-batten homes. Afterward, I attempted to read Sandy my BlessBack letter, but there was no getting through it. I was too emotional. I gave it to Sandy to read silently. We talked about the memories I had written about — the cookie jar she gave me for my bridal shower and its countless repairs because our sons wouldn't let me throw it away. Many of the things I had written, she did not remember. But for me, the memories of her kindness had never gone away. She was someone in my past whom I had never forgotten and I wanted her to know she had been pivotal to me becoming the "me" I am today.

I received my own BlessBack that day. Dick brought up my dad and memories of coaching Little League with him, something I had forgotten they did together. "Your dad was a wonderful, humble man," he said. "He always made sure that every boy on the team played in each game."

He told a story of the team's last game of the season and that one boy hadn't connected with the ball all season. "Your dad told him on his last up, 'Just take one swing,'" Dick said. "And wouldn't you know it. That little guy won the game for us."

Dick's BlessBack was a honey moment, filled with a warm glow from a good memory of Dad after he had been gone nearly a decade. My heart was resuscitated with the aroma of the world's kindest soul. It reminded me, too, of whose daughter I was and the goal of this girl: To be kind.

You may never know how your time, effort, and energy affect another person or an organization. Don't let "I'm going to" turn into "I never did." Go out on a limb, as Mark Twain said. "It's where the fruit is."

No act of kindness,
no matter how small,
is ever wasted.

— Aesop
Notes From a Traveler Afar

CHAPTER FIFTEEN

Give a BlessBack Through Gifts

I've learned that you shouldn't go through life
with a catcher's mitt on both hands;
you need to be able to throw something back.

— Maya Angelou

Whether we BlessBack through words, actions or gifts, the intent is still the same: We are giving a gift from our hearts.

Mary Bostrom taught math at Faribault's Shattuck-St. Mary's School in Minnesota in the '07-'08 school year. The headmaster told the staff in September to take time to help one another. At the end of the year, he bought sixty five-dollar Starbucks cards and during the wrap-up session after finals week put them at the front of the room. He invited teachers to give one to another teacher and thank him or her for a specific thing that person had done to help another.

One teacher thanked another for filling in when her father died. Another teacher had helped with babysitting. Another person received thanks for always saying "Yes!" when asked to help with any co-curricular activity.

"The teachers were surprised that others had noticed their actions," Mary said. "It was an uplifting time for us and made us realize how much we each played a part in each other's successful school year."

Gift-givers are those rare breeds who love to surprise us. They are creative and help us escape our circumstances, whether we're facing a hard school year as a teacher or working on a project that has us overwhelmed. They help us celebrate our achievements and change our outlook.

Kris Mestad is an artist who enjoys using his talents to capture people's special memories. He tells his story here:

"I thought it would mean a lot to my Uncle Orv to capture the memory of his grandparents' farmstead in Iowa, where he enjoyed many summers while growing up. I was limited, relying on an old blurry photo that lacked the detail that I prefer to use as a reference for a drawing. The blurriness forced me to draw a more interpretive drawing as I tried to envision the detail and transfer it to the drawing. As is the case when drawing other landscapes, I became curious about the different features that I was capturing. I envisioned myself playing hide-and-seek in the barn's attic or riding in that cute old horse-drawn buggy while traveling on a rustic road into town.

"I framed the drawing and eagerly sent it off to my uncle with a special note from me.

"A few weeks later, I received a letter from Uncle Orv that he had received it. He expressed his surprise and gratitude for my capturing one of his special memories of his childhood. Below are some highlights from his letter."

Dear Kris,

Your drawing of the Mestad barn ... what a real treasure to me and what memories came flooding forth. Your dad, Kris, probably told you the "hollow" was too lonesome for him, but the fascinations of getting all the hay in the barn by horsepower, and the antics of 'ol Uncle George, etc. seem to take me back each summer. In fact, I found a card photo that I'm including that I have hung in my study for a couple of years as a reminder, but now your beautiful drawing will replace that greeting card and the drawing puts real class to those fond memories. My deep thanks to you, Kris!

Image courtesy of Kris Mestad

Kris' uncle, at eighty-eight, is a successful man and has led an accomplished life, but he told Kris, "My grandparents were poor farmers, yet when I look back, I know now that they knew they were rich and had everything."

Kris' gift was more than a drawing. It took his uncle to where memories awakened and filled him again with discoveries he made at the farm. Though his uncle had every material possession, the drawing gave him something to remember, something that money could not buy: nostalgia, longing, the smell of hay and being a boy on a farm. By Kris' giving of gratitude, he caused a gratitude moment in his uncle, something that repeats every time Uncle Orv walks into his study and sees the picture Kris took the time to draw.

"Drawing the barn I felt connected, nephew to uncle," Kris said. "I encourage anyone to use their talents to do a BlessBack. It can be so freeing to do this one thing."

MY FAVORITE THINGS

The 88th Street Pussycats went to Cheryl's cabin in the spring of

March 2009. After a meander at a winery, we explored shops and made our way back to her cabin on Saturday night, got into our comfy clothes and started telling stories about our childhood together. We laughed until we cried and then the conversation turned serious. We started talking about Sue's mother-in-law, Mae, who had just turned eighty, and how she celebrated her birthday with a sense of humor. Sue recounted the story: "We got to her house and as we walked to her back door to enter, I saw she had scattered crutches, a walker, a cane, and a heating pad in her shrubbery." Sue and her family laughed as they knocked on the door, only to have her mother-in-law greet everyone with her arm in a sling.

"Mae is my inspiration because she walks with joy and a bounce in her step as she ages," Sue said.

We told each other who inspires us. Cheryl was the last to speak.

She left the room and came back in with big empty shopping bags in red, lime, yellow and orange. "I have something for you," she said, setting them at our feet. "A bag to hold my favorite things." She started to cry. "You guys are the Maes in my life. Above all my friends, I count you all as my most treasured friends. You and our memories together are so meaningful."

For the next hour, she played a game with us: as we made guesses as to what we knew about her, she gave us each an item to place in our bags when we got the answers right.

The first guess was easy. She has perfect nails. We each received an emery board and nail polish in her favorite color, blush.

Soon our bags filled with all sorts of things: Chocolate mints, a wall hanging, body lotion, lip balm, bracelets, and sunglasses. Lastly, she handed us a piece of paper and said, "My last gift to you is directions to my cabin because I hope you'll all come back again." It was clear that we, too, were Cheryl's favorite things.

After hugs of thankfulness, we put on our garb and piled in front of the bathroom mirror and someone snapped a picture. Aside from our oversized sunglasses, we looked the same on the outside, but inside, Cheryl had changed us with her BlessBack gifts. As I looked in the mirror, I saw the beauty in our acceptance of each other's similarities and differences. Their harmonies warmed me. Somewhere in our early years,

Great friendships are a keepsake, worth taking care of.

we had recognized our need of each other's talents and personalities and how, if we let ourselves be real with one another, we could help each other along life's way. Great friendships are a keepsake, worth taking care of. All of these thoughts came because Cheryl expressed her BlessBack in her favorite language. Love, by way of gift-giving.

In gift-giving, you will need to plan or outline your gesture of thanks, just as you BlessBack with letter-writing.

Kris let his creative juices flow before he put pencil to sketch pad. His outline involved placing himself in the photograph and imaging what his uncle saw at the old homestead.

Cheryl, too, planned her BlessBack by thinking about her favorite things, things that turned her gift into a game of memories.

The pre-work, the thinking about the BlessBack gift before giving them, is just as important as the process of giving the gifts. As we creatively prepare our BlessBack, our focus and intent is on how to connect with our receivers. Find that card that only they "get;" bring back memories with that special item from their past; something handmade — it's all fed with love.

Your gifts can be large, small, handmade, store-bought, or one-of-a-kind. They can be practical, whimsical, permanent, temporary, consumable, or lasting. The point is to give what fits your pocketbook, time, resources, and most of all, you and what you want to say.

We'll always have Paris.

— Rick Blaine in Casablanca
Notes From a Traveler Afar

CHAPTER SIXTEEN

A BlessBack Meal

Gratitude can turn a meal into a feast,
a house into a home,
a stranger into a friend.

— Melody Beattie

In the time-travel comedy *Kate and Leopold,* Hugh Jackman played a nineteenth-century duke who landed in Kate's twenty-first century Manhattan apartment. After several futile attempts at stabbing his fork into his overdone TV dinner, Leopold said in his upper-crust British accent, "May I have the next course?"

"There is no next course," Kate, played by Meg Ryan, replied dryly.

Leopold set down his fork and calmly said, "Where I come from, the meal is the result of reflection and study. Menus are prepared in advance, timed to perfection. It is said that without the culinary arts, reality would be unbearable."

Food's textures, spices, vegetables and sauces enhance our days. Nothing nourishes and refreshes like a delicious meal surrounded by people we love, a disregard for the racing of the clock, being in the present moment and participating in great conversation. The English word *companion* comes to us from the Latin *com* "with" and *panis* "bread," meaning "with whom one shares bread." In Spanish, it's *companero*, in French, *copain* and Italian, *compagno*; all suggesting that a meal time is for sharing food in the company of our friends.

My favorite companion meal was in September 2004 and shared with my husband on our twenty-fifth anniversary. I have always wanted to eat a meal on the deck of a lighthouse and that is what we did.

To get to Point Reyes, thirty miles north of San Francisco, is no small jaunt. With every switchback on Highway 1, I felt like with the next turn, we would reach our destination, but we didn't. On and on we went, through vast rolling hills and little villages. Eventually, houses and towns started to recede, replaced with pockets of fog and cows peppering well-worn pastures.

Finally, we reached Oyster Company Road. As we drove on the lane of crushed oyster shells, I wondered if we had accidentally entered someone's property. But soon we arrived at the lighthouse's parking lot. I got out, inhaled the thick, moist sea air, and noticed our rental car's tires had turned white from the dust of the shell road.

As I descended the three hundred stairs cut from the cliff's face to get down to the lighthouse, I hoped the fog had cleared so I would be able to see the views.

With the exception of the visitor store's employee, we had the place to ourselves. We climbed onto the galley deck and the ground clouds had vanished. A panoramic view of land and sea opened up before us. I peered down three hundred feet to the water and couldn't help but wonder how Sir Francis Drake had found a way to land here in 1579. The shoreline's stalagmite shards of rock, without a lighthouse above, would have easily splintered a ship.

Rick pulled out our picnic: a baguette, some cheese, grapes, and a bottle of wine from Napa Valley. With the crashing waves beneath us, the breathtaking views, and wind whipping my hair into a truly unruly mess, my husband and I separated ourselves from the world. Perched some thirty stories above the Pacific at land's end, I thought about the English explorer as he tangoed the seas.

In 1979, Rick and I had set sail in marriage and at our silver mark of twenty-five years, we discovered we had many reasons to continue on in our journey. As we ate our picnic lunch, we reminisced about our life, about the places we'd lived, people we had met through the years, funny stories that we shared. We gave thanks to one another for the ways in which we had become better people because we had journeyed life together. Dining in bliss and wind, we let the afternoon fade.

The Oxford Universal Dictionary traces one definition of *converse* back to 1668 as meaning "a spiritual or mental communion." As we shared moments of aesthetic beauty atop a lighthouse, there was mental communion, too, in which we recalled past moments of how much we had learned about life together because we had kept our vows.

I wept as I remembered
how often you and I
had tired the sun with talking
and sent him down the sky.

— Callimachus

The French have much to teach us about meals. Many who travel to France comment that their favorite part of the trip is experiencing the way the French linger at meals. There is little rush to shove food down in order to get to baseball games or skating practice. Evening meals last as long as the conversation does.

Growing up in Toulouse in the south of France, Isabelle and her family started the evening meal around 7 p.m., and rarely finished before 8 p.m.

> The French have much to teach us about meals... Evening meals last as long as the conversation does.

"Except for specific reasons, you don't rush a meal in France," Isabelle said. "This is when people sit around the table and have a conversation. It is the time where everyone shares their day."

In *Babette's Feast,* a refugee lands on the coast of Berlevaag, Norway. Nothing in this country resembles the one from which Babette has been driven — her beloved France. Two spinsters, whose father founded a Protestant church there, put Babette to work for twelve years as their servant and cook.[1]

But squabbling and feuding had so infiltrated the tiny town that by the time the planned celebration of the spinsters' father's birthday drew near, the small handful that remained of the Christian community was barely speaking to one another.

Babette asked the sisters if she could prepare the celebration dinner for the one-hundred-year anniversary of their father's birth. Initially, the sisters hesitated. Babette was Catholic. They wondered if mixing denominations would be okay. Eventually they agreed to let her make the meal.

Soon the day arrived and the celebrants gathered around the sisters' dining table. Babette had bought the best food and wine and prepared a feast for the ungrateful believers. She served dish after succulent dish to a feuding, silent room.

Babette knew the power of a communion table. Unknown to any of them, twelve years before arriving in Berlevaag, she had been executive chef of Café Anglais, the most expensive restaurant in Paris, and saw, day after day, that food and conversation go together like a hand fits into a glove. By creating an intimate environment through food, wine and ambiance, and given time without interruption, she created a communion table in this little Norwegian village. Those who had shouldered grudges slowly started to thaw and began to talk with those who had carried long-remembered regrets. Those who had worries released them during the communing hours. When the last candle ceased its flame, the church members had finally forgiven one another.

A meal is a meaningful way to BlessBack and, should you choose to, to read your letter of thanks, too. This is how De decided to BlessBack.

In her forties, De wanted to thank her ninth grade art teacher, Mr. Houts. His stability, kindness, and encouragement had had a profound effect on her and she wanted him to know it.

De, a foodie, invited Mr. Houts, his wife, and several other life influencers and their spouses, to a BlessBack dinner. As she decorated the table the day of the dinner, she thought about those coming and prayed blessings on them. Along the center of the table, De set her prized heart-shaped rocks. On each honoree's place setting, she laid a handwritten BlessBack letter of thanks and a piece of stationery and pen for them to take home and think about whom they wanted to thank, too.

As the candles burned late into the night, the eight people at the dinner laughed and told stories from their pasts, stories about school and former teachers. Toward evening's end, De read aloud each BlessBack letter. Here is what she wrote to Mr. Houts:

July, 2005

Dear Mr. Houts,

I want to thank you for the influence you've been on my life.

You probably didn't know that during my high school years, my parents had just divorced and my mother, whom my two younger siblings and I were living with, was going through a nervous breakdown. There was no stability in my family, no structure, no rules. Also no recognition or encouragement.

After having received a D+ in "Introduction to Art" class in ninth grade, I was apprehensive as to my career choice in graphic design.

I had many classes ahead of me, mostly taught by you. But for three years, my favorite place to be was your art class. Your encouraging words and the attention you paid to me and my progress were filling my much greater need for recognition. Without knowing it, you were the only source of positive influence to me during these crucial years.

It was especially meaningful when you would grab your keys and jingle your way over to the special locked cabinets with the "extreme art supplies" in it. What a treat! You'd come back to me with some special art gizmo in your hand that would further my skills or desire in the graphic design field.

Every student in that class felt special as you patiently spent time with them.

Thank you for that "Blessing"!
        De Ortiz Brandt
        Class of '76

De wanted Mr. Houts to know that because of his influence, now when she tried a new art medium, whether it was glass, leather, metal, fiber art, or pottery, she felt grateful to him all over again. Her words blessed, lifted and honored. De read her letters to the other honorees, speaking from the heart about how they specifically changed her life. After dinner, De showed her art teacher what she had created through the years. She received a BlessBack in return from Mr. Houts' smile and affirming words, as once again, they blessed her.

Ideal conversation must be an exchange of thought, and not,
as many of those who worry most about their shortcomings believe,
an eloquent exhibition of wit or oratory.

— Emily Post

De combined all three methods for giving a BlessBack. She wrote a letter, she made homemade stationery for each honoree to do his own BlessBack, and her meal served as a BlessBack action. If the community table appeals to you as well, here are some helpful hints:

Consider the ages of your recipients, their health, and the time of year you host your BlessBack meal. Make your receivers as comfortable as possible because they may hesitate or fear what you plan to do. Let them know why they are coming to dinner.

Pre-think the mealtime itinerary; it will decrease your stress. Determine whether you will read your letters before, during, or after the meal. De read her BlessBacks during dessert to allow people to eat their food. However, if your BlessBack is short, you may find reading your letter fits better at the beginning of the meal to generate conversation for others to talk about who influenced them.

Most of all relax and enjoy the company of your guests. As Isabelle's mother called to her family, "Tu viens a table." *Come to the table.*

It's the company, not the cooking, that makes a meal.

— Kirby Larson
Notes From a Traveler Afar

CHAPTER SEVENTEEN
The Glory Jar

Will you, won't you, will you, won't you, will you join the dance?
Will you, won't you, will you, won't you, won't you join the dance?

— The Mock Turtle's song
Lewis Carroll

When some people visit the beach, they look for empty shells. Not Camille Simmons. For thirty years, she has searched the world's sands for colored glass. An old aqua gallon-sized Ball jar holds her collection and sits on top of her breakfront. The sun makes the glass fracture into a sparkling kaleidoscope of color. The foot-tall jar stands guard over Camille's living room like a Fresnel lens. I ask Camille if I can look at her collection and together we lift the heavy jar and set it on her kitchen table near a window that overlooks Lake Michigan.

Camille turns the metal lid counter-clockwise and my shoulders shudder and ears wince from the creak of grit caught in its threads. I peer inside and see the jar has taken on the scratches of the dime-sized treasures within. Both jar and glass glisten like rock candy in the sunshine.

We each hold a handful of beach glass, sometimes called mermaid's tears, and my imagination wanders. I wonder about the cobalt one. Maybe a sailor's Milk of Magnesia bottle slipped from his hand during a midnight watch of rough-and-tumble seas. Or, a crestfallen wife on a cruise learned of her husband's betrayal and hurled her Evening in Paris perfume into the deep.

The two-toned green and yellow quarter-sized one reminds me of a '70s Teem soda bottle and I envision a careless teen, forty years ago, flinging it over the side of the SS *Badger*, Ludington's car ferry, as it traveled from Wisconsin to Michigan.

Camille holds a brown piece of sea glass. "I found this one on Victoria Island in British Columbia," she says. The glass looks like chilled root beer in a mug, half of it clear, half frosty and smooth. How long was it in the water to become so changed? She hands me two more, pink and yellow, sea glass her nephew Buster found and sent from Bangkok's beaches and Somalia's shores while he was in the navy. The pink chunk looks like rose quartz.

Some glass is harsh and rough-edged. Others are ice-chip nuggets. Each is in a different stage of transformation.

Camille's favorites are the ones she picked up while beachcombing behind the old brick bank in town where the backside of the building abuts the shore and beach glass lands on the little crests of slopped-on mortar. "I think I'm the only one who thinks to look there," she says. Camille picks up a curved inch-sized piece of green milk glass she found there. It looks like it had once started to change, but still has one jagged edge remaining. Another one from the back of the bank, molasses in color, looks as though it was once part of a maple syrup bottle. All that remains is the round handle grasp, shorn from the bottle. Its fierce point stands on guard, ready to sever a finger.

Another is smooth as polished alabaster, as though it has been slammed ashore by many an ice shove in a December storm and had finally come to a resting place in summer's sands.

"Beach glass reminds me of people," Camille says. "They come in all shapes, sizes, and colors. Each with a story."

I like Camille's metaphor. Our shared commonality is that we are human. Like the variance in glass shapes, we are in process. All are in some state, whether it's broken, healing, depressed or thriving. Some are like the green chipped milk glass with it sharp-edged jags. We are in crisis and in need of a healing touch, but we won't be hurt again: our spears stand at attention, ready to jab should someone get too close.

Life cartwheels, spins, and bruises. Few of us live on an even keel. For awhile the storms leave us alone, long enough to gain a foothold here, a handhold there. We let our guard down and the wind rustles the water to a high sea roar. Soon we're jostled in the liquid abyss again, as life's elements lob hurricanes and earthquakes.

A woman guesting on a reality TV show said that she was too ugly to be seen and she refused to go outside. Soap opera characters were her closest friends.

A friend told me her daughter went to join friends on a boat ride. Just before hopping aboard, one of the friends shouted from the dock, "Are you sure the boat will stay afloat if she joins us?" The icicle words stabbed this sweet young girl. She came home and told her mom she wants to drop out of school. She's thirteen.

Life's unpredictables shake us. They whirl us fathoms deep, slam us against rocks. We come up for air but not without our souls bearing battering marks. A shared heart guarantees a hurt one. A shared idea returns a rejection. Brian Friel depicts that left-out feeling perfectly in his play, *Translations*. "I'd always be an outsider here, wouldn't I? I may learn the password, but the language of the tribe will always elude me, won't it? The private core will always be ... hermetic, won't it?"[1]

We didn't start the fire, Billy Joel sings, but we spread it when we cross the bridge from curiosity to judgment within seconds of meeting someone. We slay with our words. Benjamin Franklin was right: The eyes of other people ruin us.

And we wonder why we can't stay healed.

Julie Andrews suggested we look back; at least she did as Maria when she sang to Christopher Plummer in *The Sound of Music*.

In misty blue shadows inside Captain von Trapp's Austrian gazebo, she sang, "Nothing comes from nothing. Nothing ever could. But somewhere in my youth or childhood, I must have done something good."

No matter our history, at life's beginning we were innocent, tiny clipped-belly-buttons of goodness. That goodness came from something and no matter how the world squashes, buries, shoves us, goodness will exist because Goodness has always existed.

The more you and I let Goodness in, the more we reflect Goodness and our glass fragments beautify the Glory Jar. Goodness begins to heal our stuck places, our bruises, our sharp edges in little ways when we receive and give goodness. When we grow and cultivate gratitude, the feelings generated are like a "vaccine, an antitoxin, and an antiseptic," said John Henry Jowett.

The more loved we feel, the more we see Goodness exists in others. People suddenly become visible creatures of value and we can tell them what we see in them. And when we do, Goodness ripples.

You and I. We're part of the human tribe. We can live in an intentionally-conscious state of purity and goodness, where words don't injure but instead give someone a good day.

The more loved we feel, the more we see Goodness exists in others.

In response to a request from a fifth grader to submit his favorite poem to a class project called *Poems for Life,* Mario Cuomo sent a quotation from Edwin Markham's poem *Outwitted:*

> He drew a circle that shut me out,
> Heretic, rebel, a thing to flout.
> Heretic, rebel, a thing to flout.
> We drew a circle that took him in![2]

It's springtime as I write this. Yellow bonnets have burst from the ground and my friend, Lynn — the one who planted my garden in trade for my painting rooms in her house — and her image of mending fences is on my mind. The imagery reminds me of the opportunity each of us has to change someone. Today or tomorrow, the choice is ours.

Ask yourself when you hesitate to give goodness: "Does this mend matter?" If the person you are thinking about died tomorrow, will you think, "I'm glad I gave her a BlessBack" or will it leave you wishing you had? Your mends, slathered on and intentional, matter. Especially when given by you.

Just before I left Camille's house and her jar of beach glass, I asked which piece she liked best. "I couldn't possibly decide," she said. "Each one of them is my favorite."

And you are mine. By giving of yourself and taking the time to read this book, you have given your first BlessBack. I am silenced in gratitude by your taking the time to read it.

By now, you know a good bit more about gratitude. You know that if you continue to practice showing thanks to your life influencers, you can live your life whole. Live as a role model to someone today so that another's future is different. Live your life thinking today may be the day you are the answer to someone's prayer from a century ago. These empowering forward-thinking ideas will make you live with a different outlook, a BlessBack outlook. Make yourself into a BlessBack point-of-light, both in giving and in living life, in being and becoming. Let BlessBack delight you. Let its indulgence repurpose your life.

> *Live your life thinking today may be the day you are the answer to someone's prayer from a century ago.*

Most of you know shālôm means "peace." But shālôm in Hebrew has a deeper meaning, one I want to bestow as a BlessBack to you as we go from here. At its root, it means completeness, wholeness, harmony and fulfillment. It suggests "unimpaired relationships with others and fulfillment in one's undertakings."[3]

As we leave each other, my wish and hope is that you feel filled to the brim with knowing what an important person you are, right here, right now. You've put your brave on, learned what you needed to live a blessing life.

Join me and the others who have gone before you. I'm here, championing you to stay aboard this amazing journey. Together, let's continue the ride and change our individual worlds with our BlessBacks.

Go, in shālôm. This life of yours is a BlessBack life, meant only for you. For it is you who will make your world look different.
For it is you who will make all the difference in the world.

Each of you I want you to get out there and walk — better yet, run!
— on the road God called you to travel.
I don't want any of you sitting around on your hands
I don't want anyone strolling off, down some path that goes nowhere
And mark that you do this with humility and discipline —
not in fits and starts,
but steadily,
pouring yourselves out for each other
in acts of love,
alert at noticing differences
and quick at mending fences.

— Paul, in a letter to friends in Ephesus

APPENDIX

120 Additional Ways
to BlessBack

Appendix A
BlessBack With Words

Here are some additional ideas to spark your imagination with delivering your BlessBack letter.

WRITTEN

1. Share your BlessBack stories and thoughts on the Web site, www.blessback.com.

2. Write a short story about the recipient that explains to whom you are thankful for and send him or her the story.

3. Personalize the materials. Use custom stationery adorned with stamped art or pre-printed graphics, or print a photo at five or ten percent of its original intensity on regular printer paper and write your letter on top of the background image. Or, scan a photo of your life influencer and make it into a postage stamp using usps.com or your favorite online photo store, then use it to send your letter to the person.

4. Make a short gratitude journal or scrapbook about the recipient. Use illustrations, photos, and stickers, and include your heartfelt words of appreciation.

5. Create a poem about your experience/feelings regarding your life influencer. Try Haiku.

6. Create a small crossword puzzle or an acrostic poem based on your memories.

7. Blog about your recipient, living, deceased, or MIA, and how they contributed to your life's journey.

8. Give letters to teachers/coaches/mentors who meant a lot to you. Include a photo, perhaps of you in uniform or pictures from when you knew your recipient.

9. Make a BlessBack jar or box. Use a small jelly jar and decorate it or buy a small antique tin box. Fill with slips of papers that include how you feel about your recipient and why you appreciate him or her.

ORAL

10. Give a living eulogy party in honor of your friend.

11. Write and present a toast about the couple's specialness for a wedding or anniversary.

12. Write a song about your recipient's influence.

13. Write and deliver a party toast with the "why" this person is in your life.

14. Invite your recipient to "a special place for a special moment" and say your BlessBack face-to-face.

15. Record your voice electronically or digitally on a tape or CD and present it to your friend.

VISUAL

16. Create a DVD of thanks to your recipient and present it to her.

17. Record your thoughts as if you were talking to your friend, telling of his or her impact on your life. Burn it to a DVD for a present.

18. Create a slide show using PowerPoint, using pictures, mementos, souvenirs, yearbooks, old newspaper clippings, and transform it into a DVD of memories for your influencer.

Appendix B
BlessBack Acts

ADVENTURE

19. Take someone fishing by a creek or by boat. Hide a BlessBack letter in a creel or tackle box for discovery.

20. Visit the town where your recipient influenced you. Find that special place — the old homestead, the movie theatre, park, tower chimes — where you share the most memories to read your letter.

21. Plan an event of a favorite outdoor activity your recipient likes to do such as going for a boat ride, riding in a convertible or on a motorcycle, horseback riding, bird watching, biking, hiking, sledding, dog sledding, and read your BlessBack during your time together.

22. Rent a special vehicle such as a Hummer or sports car for the day and go for a ride. Give your friend a BlessBack letter from the glove compartment and read it in a special place that holds meaning for both you and your recipient.

23. Go skydiving — read the letter before you take off and create a memory together.

24. Go snorkeling. Hide your laminated BlessBack letter underwater in a treasure chest for your recipient to find.

25. Rent canoes and paddle to a local beach or island. Swim, picnic and investigate the island to find the "buried treasure" letter you hid earlier.

26. Rent a cabin, cottage, or beach house and play a game or watch a favorite movie from years gone by that has a special meaning for your recipient.

27. If the theater is part of your memories of your recipient, attend a play. Have someone take your picture together with your friend. Later, frame the program, tickets and photo and give it to your recipient.

28. Fly or drive to an event your recipient would enjoy such as a car show, a quilt show or an antiques show.

29. Make a meal or special dessert or food gift for your friend – or create it with them to cook up something special.
30. Send cookies to someone in the military and express your specific thanks.
31. Give your friend a mani-pedi.
32. Give a shoulder, foot or hand massage.

VOLUNTEER

33. Volunteer for an organization from which you have benefited or use your circumstances to help others who are in a situation in which you once found yourself.
34. Fill a bottle with spare change and use it to send a single mother's child to a favorite camp.
35. Make a donation of time or money to your illuminator's favorite charity, in their name.

EVENTS

Events can run the gamut from a back-yard barbecue to an all-out celebration on a rented island in the Caribbean. You decide the focus, budget and scope of the gathering. The main goal though, is simply to BlessBack the illuminator.

36. Spa Day — Hire a masseuse and have a Spa Day at your home for those whom you want to BlessBack. Prepare lunch ahead or order box lunches. Read your BlessBack letters to your illuminators as they are pampered.
37. Family Reunion — When coordinating the reunion, ask those attending to write a short BlessBack letter about another relative, special to them, who is also attending. Include specific examples of what the recipient did or said and the effects on the writer. During the reunion, read the BlessBack notes. This creates an opportunity for distant relatives to get to know each other better and to bring the family closer together.

38. "This is Your Life" party — A "Living Eulogy" or "Alive" party honors the individual (or perhaps it's a couple). Those invited tell a story about the honored guest(s). Encourage guests to read their stories aloud during the party. Provide a large envelope for recipients to store and take home their BlessBack letters.

39. Give a BlessBack to a retailer or restaurant in your community known for its charitable heart by organizing a "Buy Day" when you and your friends shop or eat together at their establishment. Make sure the manager or owner hears why you are there.

40. Host a golf/tennis/fishing outing — Have guests write BlessBack notes with details of how the honoree affected their lives. Make a themed container for the letters as a gift, or slice old tennis balls, racquetballs and put the notes inside.

41. Graduation party — This is a graduation party with a twist: the graduate honors key invited guests with a short BlessBack note or, more spontaneously, tells how guests helped change his or her life. Another option for the graduate is to write a BlessBack in the thank-you note after the party.

42. Birthday party — Ask the invited guests to bring a note or a letter telling the guest of honor what he or she did or said and how it helped the guest's life. Give a special container for the honoree to store the letters.

43. Wedding reception thanks — the bride and groom prepare BlessBack notes to key guests ahead of time. Tie the notes on the backs of guests' chairs or on guests' plates. Another option is for the couple to write BlessBacks in their thank-you notes.

44. "Over the Top" gathering — Take your BlessBack honorees on a lake or riverboat cruise, to a resort, ranch, spa or retreat center. Hire an event planner to take care of the decorations, entertainment, food, hospitality, lodging, etc. Pamper guests and write each one a letter saying what they did or said and how their actions affected your life.

EXPERIENCES

These are gifts that you purchase for your recipients but ones in which you do not participate. Ask recipients' friends or relatives to find out what he or she likes to do. Remember to BlessBack within your budget. Your gesture will be meaningful because it comes from your heart.

45. Rent them a unique car for a day, classic or roadster.
46. Rent them a cabin in the woods, beach house or mountain villa for a weekend.
47. Hire a limo to drive them to a restaurant and/or a show.
48. Hire a personal chef for a meal, a day or a week's worth of food.
49. Give your friend a night or weekend at a bed and breakfast.
50. Give a gift to a spa or salon.
51. Give gourmet cooking lessons.
52. Give dance lessons.
53. Give computer lessons.
54. Give tickets to a show or game.
55. Give photography or digital photography lessons.

Appendix C
BlessBack With Gifts

56. Donate to a cause — Send a note telling of your donation in your recipients' names to let them know of your appreciation.

57. Adopt-a-? — Some organizations use an "adoption" model to raise money to care for parks, historic restorations, zoo animals, and other projects. Donate in your friend's name and commemorate it with a special note of thanks with the photo of what was adopted and why.

58. Gift certificate — Check for clues as to your friend's interests: hardware, sporting goods, kitchen/gourmet, sweets, etc.

59. Airline miles — Transfer your frequent flier points.

60. Themed gift baskets — Fill the basket's contents or have it done professionally. Tuck a note or letter inside that expresses your gratitude. For example: Game/puzzle basket: include pencils and note pads, Sudoku, deck of cards from their favorite place, their favorite games, cryptograms, and crossword dictionary.

61. Garden basket: include options such as perennials, a wind chime, garden décor, gloves, a hand tool, garden marker, small watering can, etc.

62. Golf basket: include tees, balls, a towel, divot repairer, glove. Add a gift certificate for a round at their favorite course.

63. Aromatherapy basket: include essential oils, diffusers, candles and matches or a lighter.

64. Auto basket: include bucket, soap, chamois cloth, bug remover, window cleaner, car wash or detailing coupon, a magazine subscription and a small replica of their favorite vehicle.

65. Sewing basket: include a pair of small and/or large scissors, quality colorful thread, a seam ripper, needles, pins, or vintage sewing goods wrapped in beautiful fabric.

66. Beach bag: include sunblock, portable beach chair, beach towel, sunglasses and a hat. Add a map to the local beaches.

67. Bird basket: include a pen, journal, a state-specific field guide, and a pair of binoculars. Include a bird magazine or map to local birding sites.

68. State goodie basket: A Minnesota basket could include wild rice, a cast loon, honey, a book by a Minnesota author, a Lake Superior agate, a Honeycrisp apple, or seeds of a flower/plant developed here, tickets to either the F. Scott Fitzgerald or the Guthrie theaters, or lunch at the Mall of America ... you get the picture.

69. Fishing basket: whether fly or spin cast fishing, all fishermen and women enjoy some extra goodies. Include artificial bait/lures specific to the type of fish they prefer, bobbers, sinkers, extra line, clippers, a hat (with all the items attached), etc. Include some magazines to get them ready for the season.

70. Food gifts: almost everyone enjoys good food. From a simple purchased cookie to an elaborate catered dinner, your friends are sure to relish this gift. In your BlessBack note, tell them how their kindness has helped you.

71. Personalized edibles: a cake, pie, cupcake, or cookie inscribed with "thank you!"

72. Chocolate assortment: hand-select an assortment of chocolates and chocolate-covered pretzels, nuts, cherries.

73. Baked goods: select their favorite item in different flavors, shapes or colors.

74. Breakfast in bed, a picnic lunch or a catered dinner.

75. Specialty-food baskets: fill a basket with a fabulous assortment of gifts compiled by you or a professional. Mix 'n match spices, nuts, candies, fruit, wine, tea, coffee, condiments (specialty sauces, vinaigrettes, rubs, oils), special diet goodies, cheese and crackers, baked goods or local foods.

HERE ARE SOME MORE BASKET-THEMED IDEAS:

76. Tea basket: add a teapot, a couple of china cups and saucers, a tea cozy, loose tea, tea strainer, tea biscuits or give a gift certificate to your friend's favorite afternoon tea shop or café.

77. A wine basket could include a cork screw, crackers and cheeses, cheese slicer and cutting board along with a bottle from your friend's birth year.

78. A barbecue basket might have grill tools, spices and rubs, apple wood chips or a cedar grill plank, a book of grilling recipes, or a gift certificate for a fresh cut of meat, poultry or fish from your local meat market.

79. For knitters: buy some knitting needles, a knitting bag, a book on knitting styles and trends, and a gift certificate to a yarn store.

80. A cook might appreciate a large stainless or ceramic mixing bowl filled with special spices, oils, vinegars, hot pads, specialty tools or a cookbook of favorite foods. Tuck your note inside.

OTHER IDEAS:

81. Gifts and services, like a nice blanket or warm wrap in your friend's favorite color or theme, or

82. Have a photo of their pet put on a T-shirt or coffee cup.

83. Give a membership to a local museum, zoo, art institute, history center, or arboretum.

84. Purchase flowers from a local florist to be delivered once a month.

85. Hire a personal chef for a day, week or month for your friend.

86. Send a cleaning person for a day for house/car/boat/spring or fall cleaning.

87. Give a gift certificate for a handyperson service to start or finish that project around the house.

88. Personalized gifts such as stationery: if your friend enjoys writing, stationery, a fountain pen and stamps, makes a great gift.

89. Give a leather or bound journal, special pen, and colored marker set to your friend who likes to write, draw, doodle or journal.

90. Give clothing or accessories: T-shirts and sweatshirts with a quote that your recipient used to say.

91. Frozen meals, homemade vinaigrettes, oil, wine, beer, salsa, or dried herbs are unique homemade goods. Give eggs, honey or produce from your farm or one nearby, a farmer's market or the local section of a grocery store.

92. Jewelry: Engrave a tag or charm. Engrave specific words that evoke the memory. Or, have a quote by their favorite author engraved.

93. Charm bracelet: Find out what your friend likes and is important to her. You may add only a few charms as a "starter" and she can continue the bracelet's theme herself.

94. Frame an important item for that special person — a sketch, a pencil drawing, a photo, or a letter.

95. A framed photo of you and your friend with an inscription written in gold or silver pen.

96. Have a professional take a photo of you and your friend, or of something/someone meaningful to them; frame and present it.

97. Create a capsule of saved mementos or souvenirs from your memories of your shared times with your recipient.

98. A puzzle with a photo of something you know they like (or create a custom puzzle photo), complete it, write your thanks on it, disassemble it and give it for them to assemble and see your special message.

99. A walking stick or lathed bowl made of wood from your recipient's property. Create a design, carve or wood burn your message underneath.

100. Printed golf tees, T-shirts, pens, stationery, etc. with either your own words of appreciation or a gratitude quote.

101. A lap blanket or quilt with special images of shared memories on words.

102. A single serving of silverware with customized handles, perhaps in lathe-turned specialty woods, hardened clay or beads.

103. A piece of wall art of a shared place or memory.

104. A handmade ceramic or pottery plate to commemorate your gratitude.

105. A custom-made tote or purse in your recipient's favorite colors or patterns.

Appendix D
BlessBacks in Special Circumstances

Here are some other options to get you thinking about how you might give a BlessBack in special kinds of circumstances:

106. Donate your time, money or other resources to a cause or effort which you know would interest your special person. Include a BlessBack letter stating that your donation is in memory of this person, how that person blessed you and why you chose the organization.

107. Send your BlessBack letter to a relative of the deceased, adding that you thought the relative would want to know how this life influencer impacted your life.

108. If you learn your recipient has Alzheimer's, let the spouse know the memories you have of your recipient and how the recipient changed your life.

109. Invite a relative of the deceased to dinner or for coffee and talk about how the relative played a role in your life.

110. If she is a teacher, go talk to her class about her.

111. If your recipient works at a rehabilitation center, or senior center, stage a sing-along of his favorite music.

112. If your recipient is on staff at a church, donate flowers on behalf of your pastor. Attach a card that states why you are thankful.

113. Donate favorite Bible translations or hymnals that your life influencer loved, with a card that explains that person's influence in your life.

114. If your life influencer enjoyed music or theater within his church, donate a piano tuning or money for a new stage production.

115. Teach a class with a "My Influencer" discount.

116. Obtain an autograph of their hero or celebrity crush.

117. Clean up a senior's yard.

118. Join Habitat for Humanity on a project that your life influencer would have enjoyed.

119. Form a Welcome Wagon, just like the one that welcomed you to the neighborhood and welcome the new neighbors.

120. Offer a scholarship to a camp, college, retreat, or conference, stating it is being offered on behalf of your life influencer.

Notes

Chapter One

1. Christopher Clarey, "One Last Kiss From Agassi, and It's Over," *New York Times,* September, 4, 2006, accessed January 27, 2008, http://www.nytimes.com/2006/09/04/sports/tennis/04tennis.html.

Chapter Three

1. Marion Wright Edelman, The Measure of our Success: a Letter to my Children and Yours (New York: Harper Collins, 1992), 70.

2. Stephen Marshak, Essentials of Geology (New York: W. W. Norton, 2004), 427.

3. Martha Nussbaum, Upheavals of Thought: The Intelligence of Emotions (New York: Cambridge University Press, 2007), 3.

4. Marshak, Essentials of Geology, 427.

5. Charles Dickens, Great Expectations, (London: Penguin, 1996), 102.

Chapter Four

1. Stefan Klein, *The Science of Happiness: How Our Brains Make Us Happy-and What we Can do to be Happier* (New York: Marlowe, 2002), xv.

2. Klein, *The Science of Happiness,* xv-xvi.

3. Klein, *The Science of Happiness,* xvi.

4. Sonja Lyubomirsky, *The How of Happiness: A Scientific Approach to Getting the Life You Want,* (New York: Penguin, 2007), 5.

5. Marina Krakovsky, "Science Takes on Happiness: Researchers ask: Can We Make Ourselves Happier?" *National Post,* June 9, 2007, accessed January 30, 2008, http://www.lexisnexis.com.

6. Sonja Lyubomirsky and Rene Dickerhoof, "A Construal Approach to Increasing Happiness," In J. Tagney & J. E. Maddux (eds), *Social Psychological Foundations of Clinical Psychology.* New York: Guilford, 2010.

7.   "Eight Ways Gratitude Boosts Happiness," last modified 2009, http://www.gratefulness.org/readings/eight_boosts_gratitude.htm.

8.   Sonja Lyubomirsky, "Seven Steps to New Year Happiness," *Sunday Express,* January 8, 2008, accessed August 15, 2009, http://www.sundayexpress.co.uk/posts/view/30811/Seven-steps-to-new-year-happiness.htm.

9.   Fred B. Bryant, Collette M. Smart and Scott P. King. "Using the Past to Enhance the Present: Boosting Happiness Through Positive Reminiscence," *Journal of Happiness Studies* 6 (2005): 227-260.

10.   From Bryant, et. al, 228. See V. Revere and S. S. Tobin, 1980 "Myth and Reality: The Older Person's Relationship to his Past," *International Journal of Aging and Human Development* 12.

11.   From Bryant, et. al, 228. See C. N. Lewis, 1971 "Reminiscing and Self-Concept in Old Age," *Journal of Gerontology* 26, pp. 240-243 and A. W. McMahon, Jr. and P. J. Rhudick, 1967 "Reminiscing in the aged: An Adaptational Response," in S. Levin and R. J. Kahana (eds), *Psychodynamic Studies on Aging: Creativity, Reminiscing, and Dying* (New York: International Universities Press).

12.   From Bryant, et al, 228. See R. N. Butler, 1963 "The Life Review: An Interpretation of Reminiscence in the Aged," *Psychiatry* 26 and V. Revere and S. S. Tobin, 1980 "Myth and Reality: The Older Person's Relationship to his Past," *International Journal of Aging and Human Development*, 12.

13.   From Bryant, et al, 228. See P. G. Coleman, 1974 "Measuring Reminiscence Characteristics from Conversation as Adaptive Features of Old Age," *International Journal of Aging and Human Development* 5 and M. A. Lieberman and J. M. Falk, 1971 "The Remembered Past as a Source of Data for Research on the Life Cycle," *Human Development* 14.

14.   Bryant, et al, "Using the Past" 228.

15.   Ibid, 229.

16.   Ibid, 229.

17.   Ibid, 229.

18.   Doc Childre and Howard Martin with Donna Beech. *The*

HeartMath Solution (New York: HarperOne, 2000), 6.

19. Ibid, 72.

20. Ibid, 66.

21. Childre, et al, 64-65.

22. Eva Kaplan-Leiserson, "Put Your Heart Math Into It," *American Society for Training and Development* 56 (2002) http://web. ebsco.host.com, accessed January 18, 2008.

23. Ibid.

24. Childre, et al, 69.

25. Ibid.

26. Kaplan-Leiserson, 3.

27. Stephen G. Post, "The Tradition of Agape," in *Altruism and Altruistic Love: Science, Philosophy, and Religion in Dialogue,"* Stephen G. Post, Lynn G. Underwood, Jeffrey P. Schloss, William B. Hurlbut, eds. (New York: Oxford University Press, 2002), 52.

28. Brennan Manning, *Ruthless Trust: The Ragamuffin's Path to God* (New York: HarperCollins 2002), 36.

29. Christopher Heun, "Take a Deep Breath: Biofeedback Software is Helping Students Calm Down for Better Test Performance," *Technology & Learning*, November 2006, Gale. accessed August 17, 2007.

Chapter Five

1. Robert Holden, *Happiness Now! Timeless Wisdom for Feeling Good Fast* (Carlsbad: Hay House, 2007), 33.

2. Art Carey, Give Thanks, Get a Dividend; Gratitude Makes for a Better Life," *The Philadelphia Inquirer*, April 1, 2004, accessed August 2007, www.lexisnexis.

3. Ibid.

4. Ibid.

5. Ibid.

Chapter Six

1.   Lynn G. Underwood, "The Human Experience of Compassionate Love: Conceptual Mapping and Data from Selected Studies," in *Altruism and Altruistic Love: Science, Philosophy, and Religion in Dialogue,*" Stephen G. Post, Lynn G. Underwood, Jeffrey P. Schloss, William B. Hurlbut, eds. (New York: Oxford University Press, 2002), 76.

2.   "For Lifelong Happiness Look to Okinawa," http://www. cnngo.com/tokyo/life/how-to-be-happy-h21252. accessed January 13, 2011.

3.   C. S. Lewis, *The Problem of Pain* (New York: Simon & Schuster, 1996), 131.

4.   For Droplet footage, see Discovery Channel's *Time Warp Droplet,* http://dsc.discovery.com/tv/time-warp/time-warp.html, accessed March 10, 2010.

5.   Ross Buck, "The Gratitude of Exchange and the Gratitude of Caring: A Developmental-Interactionist Perspective of Moral Emotion," in *The Psychology of Gratitude,* ed. Robert Emmons et al. (New York: Oxford University Press, 2004), 101.

6.   Stephen Post et al. *Altruism and Altruistic Love: Science, Philosophy and Religion in Dialogue,* (New York: Oxford University Press, 2002), 3.

Chapter Seven

1.   Helene Hanff, *84, Charing Cross Road* (New York: Avon Books, 1970), 9.

2.   See story in Viktor Frankl, *Man's Search for Meaning* (New York: Simon & Schuster, 1984), 102-105.

3.   Robert Solomon, "Foreword," *The Psychology of Gratitude.* Robert A Emmons et al. (New York: Oxford University Press, 2004), vii.

4.   Nelly Trocmé Hewett, in discussion, March 2008.

5.   Patrick Henry, *We Only Know Men: The Rescue of Jews in France during the Holocaust* (Washington, D.C.: The Catholic University of

America Press, 2007), 6-7.

6. Ibid, 8, 10.

7. Ibid, 10.

8. Nelly Trocmé Hewett, interview by author, March 13, 2012.

9. Ibid.

10. Ibid.

11. Ibid.

12. Pierre Sauvage, *Weapons of the Spirit* (Los Angeles: Le Chambon Foundation), 1989.

13. Philip Hallie, *Lest Innocent Blood Be Shed: The Story of the Village of Le Chambon and How Goodness Happened There* (New York: HarperCollins, 1994), 103.

14. Marek Halter, translated by Michael Bernard, *Stories of Deliverance: Speaking with Men and Women Who Rescued Jews from the Holocaust* (Peru: Carus Publishing, 1998), 237.

15. Sauvage.

16. Ibid.

17. Henry, 53.

18. Halter, 141.

19. Hallie, xvii.

20. William Hurlbut, "Introduction to Part IV," in *Altruism and Altruistic Love: Science, Philosophy and Religion in Dialogue,* (New York: Oxford University Press, 2002), 261.

21. P. Read Montague and H. C. Pearl, "For Goodness' Sake," *Nature Neuroscience* 10 (February 2007) 137. Ebsco. accessed July 15, 2008.

22. Henry, 9.

23. Henry, xx.

24. Henry, xxii.

25. Halter, dedication page.

26. Sauvage.

27. Ibid.

28. Ibid.

29. Robert Solomon, "Foreword," *The Psychology of Gratitude.* Robert A Emmons et al. eds. (New York: Oxford University Press, 2004), v.

30. Fred's story, recounted here, is told in his book, *The School That Fell from the Sky: A World War II Pilot's South Pacific Tale of Grit and Gratitude* (Bookstand Publishing, 2005).

31. Eleanor Roosevelt, *You Learn by Living* (New York: Harper & Row, 1960), 45.

Chapter Eight

1. Oprah Winfrey, "Supplement in the Best of Oprah's 'What I Know for Sure,'" *The Oprah Magazine* September 2000 (Hearst Communications, 2005), 11.

2. Nikolai Tolstoy, *Stalin's Secret War: A Startling Expose of his Crimes Against the Russian People,"* (New York: Holt, Rinehart and Winston, 1982), 53.

3. Ibid, 52.

4. Ibid, 22-23. See footnote on p. 371.

5. Ibid, 23.

6. Ibid, 26.

7. Robert Solomon, "Foreword," *The Psychology of Gratitude.* Robert A. Emmons et al. eds. (New York: Oxford University Press, 2004), vii.

8. Ibid, viii.

9. Charles Dickens, *Our Mutual Friend,* London: Penguin, 1997), 134.

10. Robert A. Emmons, *Thanks! How the New Science of Gratitude Can Make You Happier* (New York: Houghton Mifflin, 2007), 29.

11. Robert Wright, *Time Magazine,* 59 as quoted in *The Psychology*

of Gratitude. Robert A Emmons et al. eds. (New York: Oxford University Press, 2004), 20.

12.   Kristin E. Bonnie and Frans B. M. de Wall, "Primate Social Reciprocity and the Origin of Gratitude," in *The Psychology of Gratitude.* Robert A Emmons et al. eds. (New York: Oxford University Press, 2004), 213.

Chapter Nine

1.   Marianne Moore, *The Complete Poems of Marianne Moore* (New York: Penguin, 1982), 134-5.

Chapter Ten

1.   Keighla Schmidt, "Teacher Wants Letters for her 75th Birthday," *Chanhassen Villager,* March 4, 2010, 24.

Chapter Twelve

1.   "A Party from the Heart," *People* May 30, 2005, 108.

Chapter Thirteen

1.   Madeleine L'Engle, *Walking on Water: Reflections on Faith and Art* (New York: North Point Press, 1995), 34.

2.   Julian Treasure, *Sound Business,* (Gloucestershire: Management Books, 2007), 75.

3.   "A Singer's Dream," *The Gathering* (Navarre: International Ministerial Fellowship, Fall 2010), 17.

4.   Joyce Meyers, *Do it Afraid: Obeying God in the Face of Fear,* (New York: Warner Books, 1996), 2.

Chapter Sixteen

1.   Isak Dinesen, *Anecdotes of Destiny and Ehrengard,* (New York: Vintage International, 1993), 19-60.

Chapter Seventeen

1.   Brian Friel, *Translations,* (London: Faber and Faber, 1981), 48.

2.   Nightingale-Bamford School, *Poems for Life,* (New York: Simon & Schuster, 1995), 17.

3.   *Theological Wordbook of the Old Testament.*

References

Scriptural references appear on the following pages:

Page 8	Philippians 4:8, 9 and 17 (The Message)
Page 33	Galatians 6:9 (The Message)
	James 4:8 (NAS)
Page 78	Luke 6:31(NCV)
Page 84	Acts 2:45 (NIV)
Page 207	Ephesians 4:1-3 (The Message)

Made in the USA
Charleston, SC
08 September 2012